WE STAND UNITED
and other Radio Scripts

by Stephen Vincent Benét

Prose

THE BEGINNING OF WISDOM
YOUNG PEOPLE'S PRIDE
JEAN HUGUENOT
SPANISH BAYONET
JAMES SHORE'S DAUGHTER
THE DEVIL AND DANIEL WEBSTER
THIRTEEN O'CLOCK
JOHNNY PYE AND THE FOOL-KILLER
TALES BEFORE MIDNIGHT

Poetry

FIVE MEN AND POMPEY
TIGER JOY
HEAVENS AND EARTH
JOHN BROWN'S BODY
BALLADS AND POEMS
BURNING CITY
YOUNG ADVENTURE
A BOOK OF AMERICANS
(with Rosemary Benét)
NIGHTMARE AT NOON
THEY BURNED THE BOOKS
WESTERN STAR

Selected Works

VOLUME ONE: POETRY
VOLUME TWO: PROSE

Libretto

THE DEVIL AND DANIEL WEBSTER

Radio Scripts

WE STAND UNITED AND OTHER RADIO SCRIPTS

WE STAND UNITED
and other Radio Scripts

by

STEPHEN VINCENT BENÉT

with a Foreword by Norman Rosten

Decorated by Ernest Stock

FARRAR & RINEHART
INCORPORATED
New York · *Toronto*

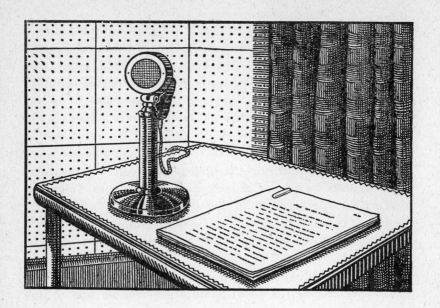

FOREWORD

The test of crisis may come to a nation or to a man, and each must meet it and be revealed. We shall not all sleep, but we shall all be changed. To Stephen Vincent Benét the test came in the shape of war. He was not found wanting, either to himself as a writer or to his country. Nor did he, as did some of his contemporaries, engage in a Hamlet-like struggle with his soul. He saw the fascist idea in all its evil and murderous stature. He knew it had to be fought. His weapon was the word, and Stephen Vincent Benét rolled up his sleeves and began turning out weapons.

Here, in this book of radio plays, are some of them. They are modern, built to specification, made for the need and cause of our time. Propaganda? That word used to be the big bogeyman of the thirties. It was trotted out as exhibit A. We were told to shun it or be damned everlastingly in the best circles. Critics and their cousins wrote long essays proving the corruption of Art. We were doomed. It was the decline of the West for certain. Well, all that is changed now. Propaganda is no longer a literary problem. It is the Idea which fights. It is artillery laying down a barrage. It helps take fortified positions. It kills and we must use it to kill if we are to survive. All this is known. Benét wrote: "I am neither afraid nor ashamed of the word propaganda. I am neither afraid nor ashamed of the fact that American writers are speaking out today for a cause in which they believe. I cannot conceive it to be the business of the writer to turn his eyes away from life because the fabric of life is shaken."

Propaganda was nothing new to him. He was always selling Americans the idea of America, and he was so engaged at the time of his death less than two years ago.

This book of radio plays is an important addition to the published works of Stephen Vincent Benét. They are plays written with anger and passion. They are eloquent without being pompous. In these pages there is something of the spirit of *John Brown's Body,* which ringed our era with a great flame of poetry. As always, the author is a teller of tales. He had given us many wonderful stories in fiction and poetry, libretto and film. There's his *Devil and Daniel Webster, Johnny Pye and the Fool-Killer, The Burning City, Thirteen O'Clock, A Book of Americans* (with Rosemary Benét), the massive and singing chorale of *Western Star,* and many others. I think this book is important because it presents the author in an entirely new medium, radio. It gives us his living words as spoken to millions of people who may never have met their great poet except for an occasional story or poem. To these new millions of listeners, his plays have brought a meaning and beauty rarely heard over the radio. To his old readers, he has proved himself equally at home on the airwaves as on the printed page. Steve Benét had that gather-ye-round quality, and the folks sure did gather when he spoke! With a wry smile, he had this to say: "I got into radio largely by accident, because I was asked to do certain things. And God knows I'm no genius at it, but I've had a lot of fun."

I'm sure he did. He took the elevator going up, stepped out into the air-cooled Inferno with a tin of Chesterfields in his pocket, chuckled at the sound and fury of the place, found a reasonably quiet corner, and got to work. For radio is an institution, which nobody can deny. Some contend it is a body of land surrounded by water. Others, more realistic merely shake their heads and tune out the commercials. A few say it can't last, but we know better. Generally, radio is a half hour of harmless sleight-of-hand during which the meaning may disappear in a mist of sound, music, or other natural causes. There is also the case in which an author himself disappeared in a fantasy music sneak. Often radio is innocent enough, with the hero shouting, "We'll come back. We strike in the night as avengers! [Burst of machine gun] I'm hit . . . keep going, Mike. Tell Mary that . . . [Whine of shell approaching and over] . . . and I'd go through it again because . . . [Plane in power dive, register, build to terrific crash] Tell her also . . . [Sudden burst of rifle fire and rocket guns] . . . and I'll always feel that way, and if she asks for my last words, tell her . . . [Music surge in, hold, bring to higher level, sustain tremolo, then rise to climax and out] . . . that's all I have to say, Mike."

There has been an occasional stirring which many of us hoped was the roused giant shaking off his chains, but it turned out to be the yawn (or echo) of an advertising agency. Into this maze of commerce, the Shangri-la of soap operas, ecstatic or grim commercials, and the man with the second hand on his watch who never grows old; into this fabled land of Time and the Product, Stephen Vincent Benét came with his simplicity. He came with the reverence of one chosen to speak to and for the people. As in his poetry and fiction, these radio pieces contain no tricks, deceptions, loud noises or other methods by which men seek to imitate grandeur. The grandeur is an honest man who will speak his truth—and none shall tamper with it. The greatness is the cause, and the word. He has kept faith with both.

I feel sure that the people of America are going to like this book. They'll like the pride of "Your Army," the soaring anger of "They Burned the Books," the tenderness and hope in "A Child is Born," and the eloquent "Prayer." They'll like the warm, familiar talk of the "Dear Adolf" series, because they, the people, get up and speak their piece—farmer, housewife, soldier, laborer, and foreign-born. We'll miss a few old flavors here—the New England smell of apples, the tang of autumn, tall tales with their folk humor and wisdom. For these are—most of them—tracts written in battle, in the hard language of battle. They are lean, without trimming. They tell us in another way what he has always told us: that as a nation we are strong, that our ancestors have given us a heritage as deep as the bone and we have fought for it and will fight again. Benét was never ashamed of his love for America, even in times when it was unfashionable to love one's country. To the cynics and unbelievers America has been merely a symbol, either great or gaudy. To Benét it has been the bread and water, the soil and air of life, a land of promise always.

In a speech before the Council on Books in Wartime, a few short months before his death, he said: "There is still a greater task, if we are great enough for it. There is the task of putting into words the old tried faiths of the past and the new hope we dimly see—the hope of the future that man can make if man wills."

The people whose faith he voiced will surely want their hope realized. To the many writers who may have felt his influence, and to younger writers like myself who remember his guidance and encouragement, he has left this challenge. We will turn to that greater task. We have his words with us forever. We will not be afraid.

Norman Rosten

CONTENTS

FOREWORD BY NORMAN ROSTEN   v

WE STAND UNITED   1

DEAR ADOLF   9
  1. Letter From a Farmer   11
  2. Letter From a Businessman   21
  3. Letter From a Working Man   30
  4. Letter From a Housewife and Mother   40
  5. Letter From an American Soldier   49
  6. Letter From a Foreign-born American   59

THANKSGIVING DAY—1941   69

A TIME TO REAP   75

THEY BURNED THE BOOKS   97

THE UNDEFENDED BORDER   119

LISTEN TO THE PEOPLE   135

A CHILD IS BORN   155

YOUR ARMY   183

TOWARD THE CENTURY OF MODERN MAN—PRAYER   203

WE STAND UNITED

This declaration was read over the CBS Network by Raymond Massey at an America United Rally sponsored by the Council for Democracy at Carnegie Hall Wednesday evening, November 6, 1940.

The program was directed by Paul F. Hannah and the music was by Paul Whiteman.

WE STAND UNITED

There is one great issue before us—an issue that concerns every man and every woman in the United States. I am going to talk about that issue as simply and plainly as I can. What I myself think and feel—one man speaking alone—is, and can be, of little moment. But the cause for which we are met tonight—the reason why we are here— is a momentous cause and a momentous reason. As a great American once said, from the floor of the Senate, in a time as troubled as ours, "Hear me for my cause!"

Yesterday, in this country of ours, we held an election. Fifty million Americans went to the polls and decided upon the Americans who are to lead and govern this nation for the next four years. They did not go with guns at their sides— or with despair in their hearts. They were not driven or hounded there by armed guards or secret police. They went of their own free will, believing—and sometimes bitterly— in one party or the other, but with freedom to choose between the two. I saw them—we all saw them. In barbershops and schoolhouses—in community centers and little untidy stores—all through the length and breadth of the continent they voted. It was a serious task and they took it seriously. You could see that in their faces.

I do not know how you felt about that voting—we are still so close to the heat and clamor of the campaign. But I know this for myself. The sight of those long lines of men and women, quietly waiting their turn outside the polling places—the knowledge that everywhere, all over the country, all the people, not just a few, were getting up and saying who and what they wanted—it filled me with an extraordinary pride. For it meant that democracy worked, and worked in a crisis. It is only once in four years that we see the whole people. We saw them yesterday.

I am speaking without bias of party. Had the election gone the other way, I would not alter one word of what I have said. I say and I repeat that yesterday democracy performed a great and essential act. In spite of omen abroad and turmoil at home, in obedience to the Constitution and with respect for law, the United States chose its leaders. To those who say that democracy is a failure—to those who say that all democracy must be weak, divided and corrupt—and you know the names—that is our first answer—and it is like a block of forged steel. To them we say: We have been able to do in peace what you could only do by force—we have been able to do by a mark on a piece of paper what you do by the gun and the whip. We have not been afraid of hearing both sides of a question. We have heard both sides and acted as a people. We shall never abandon that right.

Now that is a great thing to have done. It is a very great thing. And yet, in another sense, it is only a beginning. I shall try to say why that is so.

This campaign has been a very bitter one. We had better face that fact and admit it—we would never have built this country if we had not been willing to face facts. On both sides—not just on the one side—false and cruel things have been said. On both sides—not just on the one side—party spirit has gone into partisanship and partisanship into hate. The smears and the dirty stories—the lies and the rotten eggs—all the charges and countercharges of the last months —they were there and we know they were there.

In ordinary times, that doesn't matter so much. You call my candidate a horse thief and I call yours a lunatic and we both of us know it's just till election day. It's an American custom, like eating corn on the cob. And, afterwards, we settle down quite peaceably, and agree we've got a pretty good country—until next election. But these are not ordinary times.

These are not ordinary times because there is a crisis in our national life. It was not brought about by the election and it has not passed with the election. We have decided to arm as we have never armed in peacetime. We have decided to call our young men to military service as we have never called them in peacetime. We have done this because, in a year, we have seen the fall and ruin of free nations, and a new creed of barbarism on the march. We can no longer take our own way of life for granted—we know that it may be challenged. And we know this too—and know it ever more deeply—we know that freedom and democracy are not just big words mouthed by orators but the rain and the wind and the sun, the air and the light by which we breathe and live.

How shall we defend them—how shall we defend ourselves? We know one thing—Abraham Lincoln said it more than eighty years ago and he was speaking of this turbulent, endlessly seeking country of ours. He said: "A house divided against itself cannot stand." We cannot be a house divided—

divided in will, divided in interest, divided in soul. We cannot be a house divided and live.

The issue goes beyond battleships and airplanes—it goes beyond tax bills and laws—it goes into the heart and mind of every one of us. Each one of us is responsible—not one of us can shirk his own responsibility. In the troubled years to come, we must have unity and a united nation—not the blind unity of the slave state, but the deliberate unity of free men. And, if we really believe in democracy, we must begin to seek that unity now.

I know the task is hard. It is hard to put aside partisanship. It is hard to give up the easy wisecracking jeer that divides and destroys. It is hard—very hard—to have worked sincerely and wholeheartedly for a cause and to have lost. Most of all, it is hard to put aside personal prejudices. And yet we must put these things aside.

There is one essential thing. We have a great past to help us, in putting these things aside. This election, hard fought as it was, has been but a mimic battle. It has been bitter—but the struggle between Jefferson and Hamilton was bitter—and yet both men were able to labor for the good of their country. It has been bitter—but the Civil War was bitter—and yet, at the end of that war, the idol of the South, Robert E. Lee, laid down his sword forever and spent the rest of his life, not in bitterness and anger, but in working for peace and concord and a united land. That was a harder thing to do than any of us are called upon to do today. Yet he did it, and so doing, won a victory of the spirit as great as any victory he had ever won on the battlefield. Stephen A. Douglas died campaigning at the side of his old adversary, Abraham Lincoln. Let us be bold enough and free enough to follow the great examples—the men of good will and honor who put aside little ways and petty hatreds to build the American dream.

And, first of all, let us take two words we have heard a great deal of in the last two months—take them and bury them deep. The first is dictatorship and the second is appeasement. They do not apply to us—they do not apply to this nation or to the government of this nation. With God's grace and with the strength of a united people, they will never apply to this nation. Let us dig their graves here and now, with a long strong spade.

No administration that ever ran this country—not even Washington's—has done so without opposition and criticism. That is just and right and our way. But there is something which is neither reasoned opposition nor reasonable criticism—a sort of sit-down strike of the mind which says: "The score went against me. Very well, I won't play ball." If any of us—any man, any group, any class—could ever have afforded such an attitude, we cannot afford it now. We cannot afford the creeping paralysis that destroys the effective will of democracy—the paralysis carried by hate and rancor, between class and class, person and person, party and party, as plague is carried through the streets of a town. I am speaking bluntly—I know you would not wish me to speak otherwise. For this paralysis of will—this sit-down strike of the mind—has attacked and ravaged other nations. We cannot afford to let that happen here.

Let us say this much to ourselves, not only with our lips but in our hearts. Let us say this:

"I myself am a part of democracy—I myself must accept responsibility. Democracy is not merely a privilege to be enjoyed—it is a trust to keep and maintain. When by idle word and vain prejudice, I create distrust of democracy itself, by so much do I diminish all democracy. When I tell my children that all politics is a rotten machine and all politicians thieves and liars, by so much do I shake their faith in the world that they too must build. When I let loose intolerance, whether it be of race, creed or class, I am letting loose a tiger. When I spend my time vilifying and abusing a duly-elected government of the people because I did not vote for it, by so much do I weaken confidence in government by the people itself. Rich or poor, young or old, Republican or Democrat, I cannot afford these things.

"I cannot afford them because there are forces loose in the world that would wipe all democracy out. They will take my idle words and make their own case with them. They will take my halfhearted distrust, and with it sow, not merely distrust, but disunion. They will take my hate and make of it a consuming fire."

Let each one of us say: "I am an American. I intend to stay an American. I will do my best to wipe from my heart hate, rancor and political prejudice. I will sustain my government. And, through good days or bad, I will try to serve my country."

DEAR ADOLF

This is a series of six scripts prepared for the Council on Democracy by Mr. Benét and based on original letters addressed to Hitler by representative farmers, businessmen, laborers, housewives, soldiers, and foreign-born Americans.

The entire series was broadcast over the NBC Red Network on successive Sunday afternoons beginning June 21, 1942 (with the exception of July 19th), and ending August 2, 1942. The series was directed by Lester O'Keefe (with the exception of "Letter from a Foreign-born American," which was directed by William M. Sweets), was produced by Milton Krents, the music composed by Tom Bennett and the orchestra conducted by Josef Stopak.

LETTER FROM A FARMER ......read by Raymond Massey

LETTER FROM A BUSINESSMAN ....read by Melvyn Douglas

LETTER FROM A WORKING MAN ....read by James Cagney

LETTER FROM A HOUSEWIFE AND MOTHER
read by Helen Hayes

LETTER FROM AN AMERICAN SOLDIER
read by William Holden

LETTER FROM A FOREIGN-BORN AMERICAN
read by Joseph Schildkraut

1. LETTER FROM A FARMER

FARMER: Will you get me the pen and ink, mother? I want to write a letter.

Got time enough, for once. Weather looks as if it would hold.

No, I'm not going to write the boy tonight. Wrote him last week, to the camp, and told him how things were going.

He knows how it is—he was brought up on a farm. But there's lots of folks that don't know.

Got it on my mind ever since the boy went away. Kind of boiling and steaming up in me to say a few things.

No, don't want the county agent to do it, or even the President. They're all right. But this is my letter.

This is me and I want to talk to that fellow over in Germany that started all this trouble.

Want to tell him just who I am and what I'm thinking. Maybe time I did.

Got the pen, mother? Thanks. Now you just let me think
    it out.

Dear Adolf—This is me.
This is me—one American farmer.
Six million farms and over in this country, last census. Six
    million places where we can raise food for freedom.
Food for the men on the ships and the men in the planes.
Food for the boys like my boy in his soldier clothes.
Food for Ed Summers' boy on his destroyer and Gus Taub's
    boy over in the tank-plant.
Food for all kinds of folks I'll never see in my life who are
    fighting on our side.
British children and British seamen and Chinese soldiers,
    most likely, and Russians.
Shucks, I can't add 'em all up. I can't even add myself up.
    My farm's just one of six million.
But I want to say this. We're all against you, Adolf.
Every bushel of wheat in this country is against you. Every
    furrow we plowed this spring, we plowed against you.
Every time a hen lays an egg, that egg's against you. Every
    time an Iowa hog puts on another pound, that
    pound's against you.
Against you and all your works, because we don't like you
    and can't stand you and we're bound and determined
    to get rid of you, whatever it costs us all.
Ever think what that means,—to rouse up a free people,
    Adolf? Guess not.
You see, we farmers don't talk much. Never have.
You can read in the papers about us—parity prices and such
    —but that's politics, that isn't our story.
Our story's weather and land and the things that stay.
The wind around the corner of the barn and the lambs in

March, the look of a well-limed field, and the reason a man likes to grow things, the reason it's a satisfaction.

The reason a man will put up with hail and drought, blight and blizzard and cornborers—put up with them and cuss them out and fight them all his life and get through somehow—just because he's got a fool idea in his head that that's what he was born to do.

You hitched up the wrong horse when you thought that farmers can't fight, Adolf.

Farmers are used to fighting. They fight every day in the year.

There's never enough rain for a farmer, except when there's too much. There's never a good crop but there couldn't be a better. There's never cash in the bank but the tractor don't break down.

That's us. You can call us cantankerous and slow to change. You can call us independent, too, because that's what we are.

Our own government's found that out and you're going to find it out, too.

We're labor and capital—both. We've got everything to lose, if you win. And we know it.

Sure, we didn't bother about you for quite a while.

We had our own problems here, and we've been working them out—ever since triple A came in. Sure, lots of things we didn't like about triple A—at first. But we've worked it out with our government over ten years now, and they've listened to what we said. Can you say that for any of your farmers? Not that I've heard.

And meanwhile, of course, there's the work—the work that never stops.

Twelve hours a day—seven days a week—that's what work
    means to a farmer.
You can't rush it but you can't let up on it. You can't tell
    a cow not to calve because you want to go to the
    movies. You can't tell corn "Please stop growing—
    I've worked my eight hours a day and that's enough."
    Then you've got to get in the hay, you've got to get
    it in—it won't wait till Tuesday.
So, with that kind of work on our minds, we didn't pay
    undue attention to your goings-on across the water.
    Not at first.
Though we didn't like the way you took on about races
    and such—we don't ask if our neighbors are Aryans
    or what have you. We just ask if they're good neigh-
    bors.
And when you started spreading all over Europe like a mess
    of tent caterpillars, well—But it looked, for a while,
    as if other folks could do the spraying.
But you take my brother—he's a farmer too, up in the
    Northwest. He wrote me a letter awhile ago and this
    is what he says:

    voice: Four years ago when you'd bring in a can of
cream to our Farmer's Co-operative Creamery, you would
find German-American farmers and Danish-American farmers and all kinds. And they are all good farmers and good
Americans except when they have a schoolboard election.
Then the Swedes all vote for a Swede and the Germans for
    a German and so forth. Doesn't mean hard-feeling.
    Just habit.
Then, a few years ago, this Hitler starts making the world
    over again according to his own ideas. And a funny
    thing happens at the Farmer's Co-operative Creamery.

Because one day, Hodak, who is a Bohemian, gets a letter from some relations in Czechoslovakia. This relation writes things look bad over there and Czechoslovakia is going to be swallowed up by Germany.

Well, Otto Libers and Heinie Grootschnitt laugh and say it is a lot of lies. They say Hitler is a great man because he is the Fuehrer which means leader and he has no idea of hurting Bohemians.

But it turns out Hodak is right and Hitler takes Czechoslovakia and Hodak's relations and everything they've got, including their stock.

Then, later on, Hans Christiansen is in the harness shop and he pulls out a letter from a cousin in Denmark who is a farmer. He writes that they can no longer sell cream and butter to England who used to pay cash but now they got to sell it to Germany and all they get is worthless scrip.

It is only a few days after that when we hear Denmark is occupied. And Hans Christiansen does not hear any more from his cousin. He does not hear any more from his cousin at all.

And the same kind of stories come to us farmers at the creamery from France and Norway and a lot of other countries. They are not good stories to hear or pleasant to hear.

And all the time this Hitler claims he is making a United States of Europe. But I can tell him he is making a United States of America and making it right in our neighborhood.

Because we do not like to hear about stock being stolen and people being starved and folks being shot without cause. And if he could see people like Otto Libers and Heinie Grootschnitt plowing up older cultivator

shovels and other scrap iron to shoot back at him,
this Hitler would know what he had tackled when
he tackled us.

Because there aren't any German-Americans or Danish-
Americans in our neighborhood now. They are all
Americans, and they are all in this war and that is
the answer.

FARMER: Well, Adolf, that's the answer.

That's how some of us got to know what you were like.

And the rest of us—well, maybe it came with Pearl Harbor
—or even before. We'd upped our food quotas before. But Pearl Harbor and the way those Japanese
beetles acted just touched it off.

Now, we're mad.

We're mad and we're out to get you, Adolf—get you and
your pals—every one of us.

And, when we say you and your pals—we mean just that.

We mean this Mussolini that you've got cooped up in Italy
like a broody hen—that's a way for a man to act,
isn't it?—and those smart little sons of heaven that
took their farms away from the Chinese.

We don't like that kind of thing. We don't mean to stand it.
And, most of all, we'll be immortally damned if we
have it here. Sorry, mother, just lost my temper a
minute.

Want to know what we're saying—all over the country—us
farmers? This is it.

There's a woman up in New Hampshire and she says:

VOICE: "I can't fire a gun but bless you, I can keep firing
this sausage out of here for the folks that need it to fight on."

FARMER: There's a fellow over in Maryland. He's had
hard luck, as you can tell. But he says:

VOICE: "The orchard is worthless, peas suffered from drought, potatoes suffered from drought, sow had no pigs, three cows culled, pipe line rusted and busted, but I'm keeping on. I read about how our soldiers need more food from us farmers. They'll get it if I have to bust myself wide open."

FARMER: There's an acre in the South—one of many all over the South—and the sign says this on that acre:

VOICE: "I hereby dedicate this acre of my cropland, to be planted in peanuts, to James Walls, my soldier in the service of the U. S."

FARMER: There's a fellow in Kansas and he says:

VOICE: "I'll be willing to eat hard bread and drink ditch water for the soldiers that fight this war for me."

FARMER: There's a fellow who writes in to the FSA and he says:

VOICE: "I have a brother and a brother-in-law already in service now and many close friends, some of whom have already been killed. And I am willing to work for small profits so those boys may have everything they need and the best we can give them. I used to be scared of war but, I can see why men are ready to fight—yes, fight for their country and their freedom. And whatever it takes, I am ready. I want to show these dirty back-stabbers what a country of God-loving and free people can do or the last one of us die trying."

FARMER: And this is a lady down in Alabama. I'd like you to pay attention to this, Adolf. I know that kind of lady, and we've got a lot of them. And this is what she writes:

VOICE: "My husband has been ill. But I will tell you what I and two girls did in '41. We made 100 bushels of corn and a ton of peanuts, 30 bushel of peas, 20 bushel Irish potatoes, 40 bushel of sweet potatoes. A good garden, one bale of cotton, raise about 200 chickens and have plenty of eggs. Eleven months ago a friend gave us a little pig. I fed him with a spoon and last December I butchered this pig. He weigh around 400 pound. If I could get the hogs and where to fix a hog pasture I could do more. Because this is the lady's war, same as the men. And I pledge myself in '42, I will can double the amount of '41. I will raise two hogs for the boys in service, one for myself. I have Pearl Harbor wrote down on my heart."

FARMER: That's it, Adolf. That's our answer—the answer of our part of the home front.

They won't be flying "E" pennants from the silos and we won't be getting medals and decorations. But we've got Pearl Harbor written down on our hearts, Pearl Harbor and Wake Island and the names of the dead.

We'll work for them and fight the earth for them. We'll do what we're asked and more. We'll produce as we never produced before.

The government's asking for milk—125,000,000,000 pounds of milk—eight billion and a half more pounds than last year. They'll get it.

Enough milk to fill up the whole River Rhine at Emmerich, Adolf, and keep it brimming for seven and a half hours. Enough milk to float two thousand battleships like the *Bismarck*. 3,855,000 pounds more milk this year from Hunterdon County, New Jersey, alone.

Enough milk so our folks at the front and at home stay strong to fight you. Enough milk so we can ship it dried to our Allies who need it.

How's the milk in Germany, Adolf? How much are your people getting?

You promised them guns and butter. How many guns would they swap for some of our butter? How much milk are your soldiers getting on the Russian front? How much milk are their families getting—the families they left behind? Do you even know?

All over America, the Victory gardens are growing. All over the land we're raising the food for freedom.

No, it isn't an easy job. I'll be frank with you about that.

You see, we can afford to be frank. We don't have to lie to our own folks to get things done.

We've got to work harder, every farmer, because with the army and the war industries there'll be less and less help we can hire.

We've got to patch up the farm machinery and make it do because it's more important right now to make bombs to drop on you than it is to make farm machinery.

We'll get prices that may sound high but we'll make less on the year. Feed's up and labor's up. There won't be $25 hogs in this war—but we won't be slave labor afterward. We'll feel the pinch like the rest and we'll go through like the rest.

My hands are getting stiff but I can still milk. My store suit's getting old but I won't be needing it much. I take good care of my car—but I'd rather have freedom than new tires.

Why are we doing it, Adolf? Well, that's something you wouldn't understand. We like freedom.

Our government's not telling us to do this with machine guns. Our government's saying "Can you do it?" and we're saying "Twelve hours a day. Seven days a week."

My boy wrote me from his camp this spring and he said:

VOICE: "Of course I am lonesome sometimes because I miss the folks and home on the farm in the hills. I know our soil is none too rich, after use and misuse by many generations of farmers, and some of it is stony; but I know our hills are green, now. I don't know why, but I love them most when the snow drifts deep under the hemlocks and shakes down from the trees when I walk through with my gun and my dog. No time is too long to fight to keep our home in the hills safe and free."

FARMER: And I feel just the way my boy does. That's the way I feel about this country.

It's too big for puny affairs and small potatoes. It's too big for grumbling and name-calling and holding back in the pinch. And it's too immortally big for you or folks like you to meddle with or put your brand on.

We'll choke you with wheat and corn, Adolf—we'll drown you in New York State milk—we'll smother you with cotton and soybeans and roll you up in the middle of a big Wisconsin cheese.

The earth's roused up against you, Adolf—the prairies and the big plains—the black earth down in the Delta and the little hillside farms where you have to plow between the stones.

There's six million farms against you, Adolf—six million farms and their farmers—the men with the slow talk and the sunburnt backs to their necks—the women who know that a farm woman's day never ends.

And we're not a special class or a special interest. We're part of something and working for something that's bigger than any of us—something big as the sky above us and fertile as the earth underfoot.

It's called the United States, Adolf. And she was born in freedom!

[*Music swells*] That right, mother?

(CURTAIN)

2. LETTER FROM A BUSINESSMAN

BUSINESSMAN: Yes, that's the afternoon mail, Miss Smith. All signed.

Yes, I talked to Major Lempert. Going to meet him at the plant. Any other calls?

Mrs. Benson did? Well, I can't get back for dinner. The Major and I will pick up something, somewhere. He won't mind.

Yes, Miss Smith, I had lunch. You can tell Mrs. Benson I had lunch. And don't look as if I never had it. That was just last week when we got the changed specifications.

No, I don't know when I'll be through. I may sleep at the plant:

Take a letter, please, Miss Smith.

Adolf Hitler, Berchtesgaden, Germany—yes, that's right and look up the spelling.

I've had this letter on my mind for quite a while. Ever since
    the boy got into the Air Force. Well, he's a good boy
    and—
All right—take this letter.

Dear Adolf—this is me.
This is me—one American businessman—J. B. Benson of
    Benson and Company.
I run one plant in one town in a place called the U.S.A.
I'm 49 years old, three children and a dog. Been in the
    manufacturing business ever since I got out of the
    last war. Believe in it, too.
I'm a church member and a Rotarian and a lodge member.
    In politics I usually vote the straight ticket though,
    once in a while, I'll split it for a good man.
Sometimes Mrs. Benson says that's stubborn of me. Some-
    times she says I'm broad-minded. It all depends, I say.
I'm vice-president of the Chamber of Commerce, in my
    town. I help run the Community Chest.
And there are thousands like me all over this country. Just
    the plain, ordinary businessmen who sit at table 24
    at the convention dinners and are out on the end of
    the row when they take the group photograph.
That's why I'm taking time off to say "We're all against you,
    Adolf."
The businessmen—the manufacturers—the industrialists—
    the men who designed and put together the whole
    big plant of America—we're moving against you.
We're against you and we're out to lick you, come hell or
    high water.
It's a big job and we know that. But we make everything
    in this country from electric toasters to suspension

bridges. And, if we don't know how, at first, we scratch around and find out.

We make gadgets and dofunnies and jiggers—and things that last. We're crazy about three-ton presses and automatic lighters, about cash registers that ring bells at you and cranes that pick up tons of steel. We're crazy about feeding stuff in at one end of an assembly line and having a car drive out on its own power at the other. We're crazy about jigs and dies and tools that make tools.

And that's why this war is up our alley, Adolf. Because it's mechanized war. You said it yourself.

We admit, you got a head start. You were making machine guns while we were making washing machines. You were making tanks while we were making pleasure cars. We could have converted earlier and maybe we should have. But we were making peace while you were making war. Well, that changed at Pearl Harbor.

Now you've given American business the biggest order of its life. You've taken the everlasting lid off our production. We understand your market's war, Adolf —well, we mean to see that market glutted. You started fooling around with tools of death. We're toolmakers by trade. We've delivered a few samples already—ask Tokyo and Rumania. But the real mass production's just starting on the way.

It's in the plants and on the freight cars and trucks. It's crossing the oceans in convoy. It's pouring from thousands of factories, all over America. The soldiers we send to fight you are going to be as well-equipped as American skill can manage. There are typefounders making tank guns, locomotive works making barbettes, tire companies making leakproof gas tanks. It's boiling in the converters and humming over the power lines. It's being stamped out and welded and machined and finished—and marked with your address.

There are plants a mile long that do nothing, night and day, but work at it. There are little shops that do nothing, night and day, but work at it. There's a fellow who used to make musical cigarette boxes. He's making airplane parts. There's a fellow who used to make children's slippers. He's making canvas saddlebags for the Army. There's General Motors and Ford, Allis-Chalmers and Bethlehem Steel, Gary and Hartford, Pittsburgh and Youngstown, the River Rouge and Willow Run. And there are hundreds of plants you never even heard of. But they're turning the stuff out, now.

Why? Well, there's just one reason why—

A COOL, THOUGHTFUL VOICE: "Our resources will beat the Axis. But, if we don't hammer those resources into tools and planes and tanks in time, we might just as well be buried with our unused resources."

NARRATOR: No, that wasn't our government, Adolf. That was a manufacturer in Louisville, Kentucky. And that's why the wheels are rolling. That's why cornfields turn into tank plants. That's why we build the plants a mile long. Want to hear another? Well, this is the most respected man in my town, talking to our Chamber of Commerce.

A CONSIDERED VOICE: "Gentlemen, war business is not good business. It's hard to get and it's harder to get a profit on it. It's as full of troubles as Pandora's box. I'm taking all I can get, because, if American business does not make a success of this job, it will never get the chance to fail at another."

NARRATOR: That's our own men—talking horse sense. We've heard what you did to your businessmen. We've heard what you did to Thyssen and Hugenberg and the businessmen of Germany. They backed you or they didn't— but, whether they backed you or whether they didn't, you stole them blind. You broke the labor unions first—and they thought that was fine. But then you broke *them*, and you broke them to powder. And the only business that's running in Germany today is your gang's business, Adolf. Well, that isn't the way we want it here.

Sure—some of us thought for a while that we could do business with you, even if you conquered all Europe. But we don't think that any more.

You can't do business with a man who doesn't know the meaning of a contract. You can't do business with a firm who swears they'll do one thing one day and does just the opposite the next. You can't do business with a company who takes your goods on a cash basis and then pays you off in bum harmonicas. You can't do business with people whose whole idea of business is "Heads, I win. Tails, you lose."

We call those people chiselers in this country, Adolf, and when they get to be too much of a nuisance, we put them out of business. And that's just what we mean to do to you, and your friends the Japanese war lords. Because you're international chiselers—and there can't be any real business done till you're stopped.

Sure—we kick about a lot of things here. We kick about taxes and we kick about red tape. We kick about rules and regulations and we kick about government interference. We kick about questionnaires and we

kick about the New Deal. We can kick—we're free
men. Your fellows can't kick—or they're shot.
It's curious, Adolf. Not one American businessman has yet
been shot by our government because he didn't agree
with our government's policies. It's curious because,
with all that, we're making a production record now
that we never made in our lives.
It must be curious to you. But we mean to keep it that way.
And, as for our business objective—here's what one plant
manager says:
VOICE: "After a 94 per cent excess profit tax and higher
inventories, there won't be much gravy left for the stock-
holders. But that old whistle out there will still be calling
men to work after this war is over. And that is more than
some of Schicklgruber's whistles are doing right now."
NARRATOR: Yes, that's our objective, Adolf. It's a low
commercial ideal, according to your way of thinking. It isn't
geopolitics or a co-prosperity sphere. It's tied up with buying and selling, free enterprise and competition, labor and
management. And—who was that guy awhile ago who was
sure he could lick the British because they were a nation of
shopkeepers? What *was* his name? He marched into Russia,
too.
I'm not painting a rosy picture. Things are tough and
they're going to be tougher. Industries that can't con-
vert will suffer badly. Many businesses will suffer
badly. We'll all be regulated as we've never been
regulated before. Some chiselers will make undue
profits. And we'll all see many changes. But we built
the big plant and we mean to keep it working. For
the U.S.A. Not for you.
To work and to plan and to do something. To try new
things and get them done. To get the cost down and

the volume up so the ordinary man can have things that only the few could enjoy a little while ago. To make some kind of profit out of brains and skill and management. And to get the world straightened out so that people like you won't keep gumming up the world's business.

That's our hope, for what it is. But, nowadays, we don't even try to put that hope into words. We just keep on driving. Because, always, at the back of our minds, we hear—

COOL VOICE: . . . Our resources . . . But if we don't hammer those resources into tools and planes and tanks in time, we might just as well be buried with our unused resources . . .

CONSIDERED VOICE: . . . If American business does not make a success of this job, it will never get the chance to fail at another.

NARRATOR: That's what the clock keeps ticking, Adolf. That's how we see your threat to our kind of people. There are those who would try to divide and disunite us—set class against class, creed against creed, race against race, management against labor, business against government. But that's *your* game, Adolf. And we're getting on pretty fast to the very few in this country who like to play your game.

We've got a good country and we believe in it. We've got a good way of life and we believe in that. We may not spout about it much but, if we've got any sense, we know, deep down in our hearts, that, whatever we've given this country, it's given us more. And we intend to pass on those gifts to our children.

No—we won't die in battle. We'll die of coronary and Bright's and the overwork diseases—maybe a few years earlier than if you'd never been born. Well, that's all right. If you send a plane over tomorrow and lay a bomb on this plant and bury me under it —well, it was J. B. Benson's plant and he lived and died J. B. Benson, a free American.

He wasn't Henry Ford but he did all right in his line. He kicked at his government and he never broke ninety on the golf course but they liked him pretty well in his town and he paid his bills on the first. And, when he figured he owed the United States a debt, for value received, he paid it. He paid it by scratching around and getting things done that couldn't be done in less time than there was to do them. And, if there's a balance due—and there probably is—his son and his partners and the company will take over the rest of the debt and see it's paid in full.

They won't slacken and they won't tire. They won't rest and they won't fight about objectives. They'll keep the wheels humming and the drafting boards busy and the plant turning out the stuff till the iron-jawed Axis boys who thought J. B. Benson was a sucker and a softy yell "Uncle." For J. B. Benson worked for money and he made plenty of mistakes. But, when the pinch came, as the schoolbook says, he would not bow to tyrants. He got up on his hind feet instead and said "Let's go!" He was a Past Grand Master in the Assorted Princes of the Desert—he wore plus-fours when they were fashionable and looked like hell in them—he was proud of his children and his electric razor—he liked to broil steaks on a special outdoor grill and he made a special sauce for them that gave Mrs. Benson the willies—he'd tell you at the drop of a hat about the speech he made at the convention. But he would not bow to tyrants and he worked his head off to lick them. And that's all you need to know about J. B. Benson. Except that, living or dead, he doesn't intend to be licked.

[*In a slightly different voice*]

That's all, Miss Smith. Yes, use the company letterhead. Copy to Mussolini? No, I don't think we need to waste paper. But send one to Hirohito. And mark them both—special delivery. By bomber. Now I'd better get over to the plant.

(CURTAIN)

3 . LETTER FROM A WORKING MAN

[*Open with music and background noises of a big plant at work*]

NARRATOR: Dear Adolf—

[*Grind of a lathe*]

A VOICE: Shift number one. Machine Shop. Shift number one.

NARRATOR: Dear Adolf—

[*Thud of a mechanical hammer*]

VOICE: Shift number two. Drop Hammer. Shift number two.

NARRATOR: Dear Adolf—

[*Noise of welding*]

VOICE: Shift number three. Welding. Shift number three.

NARRATOR: Dear Adolf. We're writing you a letter and it isn't in fancy words. It's written around the clock by the working stiffs of America—the guys with grease on their faces who know what work means. It's written in steel and plastics, carborundum and tungsten, rivet buckers and drill templates, planes and guns. How about it—you guys at Raw Stores?

VOICE: O.K. Send it on to Adolf!

NARRATOR: How about it, Sheet Metal?

VOICE: Don't give us the oil. We're busy. Send it on to Adolf!

NARRATOR: How about it, Production, Inspection, Engineering?

VOICES: —on to Adolf!

NARRATOR: Experimental—Metal Bench—Finishing and Plating?

VOICE: Got no time to gab. We're busy. Send it on to Adolf!

NARRATOR: How's it coming, Final Assembly?

VOICE: Can't you read the chart, you dumb bunny? The figures keep climbing, don't they? Send them on to Adolf!

[*Music up into a big factory whistle. Tramp of men's feet. Machine noise continues in background, uninterrupted*]

NARRATOR: That's the old shift going off and the new shift coming on. And, eight hours from now, that shift will go off and another one come on. And eight hours from then —same business. Because this is an American war plant and it's making war!

A NAZI VOICE, BREAKING IN: But that is impossible, my good man. You cannot make war. Your workers only work forty hours a week. I have read it in your papers.

NARRATOR: Listen, sap, don't give me that baloney. Sure we got a forty-hour week, base pay. And wouldn't your sweated workers like to have one. But—how many hours did you work last week, in your plant, Jimmy?

A VOICE: 52.

NARRATOR: How about you, Shorty?

A VOICE: 48.

NARRATOR: Mike?

A VOICE, ITALIAN [*excitable*]: I don't know how hella da long I worka dis week till I getta da paycheck. Maybe 56, maybe 60. I know dam well I worka da overtime because we gotta rusha job and she's gotta *rush*.

NARRATOR: 48—52—60. Well, why are you doing it?

VOICE 1: Got kids. Raising 'em.

VOICE 2: I get paid for the overtime, don't I? So what?

ITALIAN VOICE: Da old woman she tella me she wanta fix uppa da house. She say, Mike, getta da lead outa your pants and work on da rusha job—da house she needsa be fix.

A FAT, AMERICAN VOICE [*breaking in*]: Just what I suspected. Just what I've always said. Apathy. Selfishness. Greed. Eyes that never look beyond the paycheck. Labor asleep at the switch. Oh dear, oh dear. Don't you realize that, while you get paid for overtime, our brave American boys are fighting and dying—

NARRATOR: You needn't tell us. We know.

We got brothers in the Army and Navy, we got sons and nephews and guys that worked at the same bench with us. We aren't spilling off about them but we aren't forgetting them. We don't like the bunk and the oil and the big words. We don't like star-spangled orations that don't add up. But we know what we're doing—and we know what they're doing. Every time we throw a switch or pull a lever—every time we set up a new job—every time the whistle blows for the new shift—we know what we're doing—over twenty million of us—and don't be fooled about that.

Did you ever sleep in what they call a "hot bed," Mister— a bed that never gets changed because, as soon as you get out of it, the guy from shift three gets in? Did you ever work in an asbestos suit in front of the hot steel? Did you ever work on high iron—did you ever climb the poles? Did you ever go down the mine shaft, in the cage, and wonder, now and then, about the guys last week who never came up from Shaft Six? Did you ever see a man's hand chewed into red pulp, just because he slipped up for a split second?

Then don't talk to us, mister. We aren't softies and we aren't pampered. We're working stiffs and we're tough.

That's where you made your mistake about us, Adolf. You thought we weren't tough. You thought dough was all we were after. And you thought we couldn't think.

Well, we're thinking now and we're thinking about this war. We aren't thinking about it in slogans—Ax the Axis and Set the Rising Sun. I guess they're all right, as advertising. But we're thinking about it like this.

A RATHER SERIOUS VOICE: I'm a mechanic. Live in Seattle. Guess I wasn't so sold on this war, at first—no, not even on the need for victory. Then I heard a broadcast listing the names and trades of twenty Norwegians, shot by the Nazis because they tried to escape to England. One of those men was a mechanic. I could imagine myself in that man's place. Perhaps he was just like me; maybe he had a family just like mine. If that could happen to a mechanic in Norway, it could happen to a mechanic in Seattle. Every time somebody grumbles about the war, I think of that mechanic in Norway. I think about him and me.

NARRATOR: Get that one? O.K. Here's a guy from New York State.

VOICE, MAYBE BRONX: I'm a radical drill operator, working in a plant that turns out vital equipment for our Navy. I work to close tolerances. My machine is intricate and requires deep concentration. I can do my work fast and efficiently for two good reasons. Peace of mind is one—we've got decent wages and working conditions and my loved ones are secure. And then there's my desire to do my share in aiding my country. That's part of it all. Well, just multiply these thoughts by millions of fellows like me.

NARRATOR: Multiply them, Adolf. Add them up. And stick this one in. Here's an electrical worker from Kansas City, writing in to his union journal.

VOICE, MIDWEST: A while ago, in these columns, we snarled "What war?" We know now "what war." It's a war in which laborer and employer must fight shoulder to shoulder or perish side by side.

NARRATOR: Here's one from an airplane plant.

OLDER VOICE: I have two sons who are in the American Army. I don't want to see them fail for lack of equipment. And here's where we're turning out the stuff. Every time I complete my particular work on an airplane assembly, I speed it on the way to my sons.

NARRATOR: And here's something just a little different. He isn't a skilled worker—he's nobody you ever heard of. He's just a rag peddler. Yes, I said rag peddler. But, over here, Adolf, even rag peddlers can have ideas of their own. And he says—

GERMAN VOICE [old]: I am an old man and an individualist. My German inheritance comes from three generations, born here in America. As a young man, I traveled through Germany and half of Europe. My trades are many but now rag peddling is my only desire.

In the dark streets and alleys, in the lawns surrounding the residences of the so-called better class, through the nerve-killing noise of industry, I make my daily trips. There I see the gambler, the stickup man, the prostitute, the worker, the businessman and all the different kinds of people what make this world. I see plenty rags of human minds. And once, in my bundle of rags, I find your book, *Mein Kampf*. I read it because I want to know what it's about.

After I finish that book of hate and nonsense, something happened inside of me. I have a strange desire to live till the biggest rag-collecting job in the world is done and I know it will be done. We will take your rags on par value, Mr. Hitler. The world will see you naked. The medals and uniforms of your Hermann Goering, the ropes of your Heinrich Himmler, and all the rags you accumulated will be collected. The rate of fear, the sufferings of your tortured Europe, will go with the swastika on the big rag pile.

Adolf, your time is gone. I want your rags. I am old and I know when things are good and when they are rotten.

NARRATOR: And now—back to another war plant and another workman.

VOICE: I have been buying war bonds with every spare dollar. I have been working on my war job with every ounce of strength. I intend to go on doing that because I know that never again will I have overtime pay or a shop committee or the right to change my job—if Hitler wins.

And he won't win, while the boys in Plant Four keep working.

NARRATOR: Get it Adolf? That's us.

More than twenty million workers, eleven million union members, all over the U.S.A. Yes, I'm talking about unions. I'm talking about C.I.O. and A.F. of L. I'm talking about every union man in this country. Because we know what you do to unions, Adolf. You don't fight them and you don't debate with them. You wipe them out hide and hair.

Over here, a union button's a union button. In Germany, now, it means your controlled Labor Front. In Japan, it never existed. In Italy—well, can you imagine a Mussul-union? There's just one thing about unions you've taught us, Adolf. They can't grow inside your New Order. They can only grow in a democracy. They can only grow on free soil.

A VOICE: Calling Local B241. Calling Local B241.

A VOICE: No answer. There's no answer.

VOICE: No answer from any local.

VOICE: No answer. Address unknown.

NAZI VOICE: All patriotic workers are now members of the Labor Front. All unions are now a part of the Labor Front. There are no other workers, no other unions.

VOICE: Hans was secretary of the local. Have you heard what happened to Hans?

VOICE: Concentration camp. Term indefinite.

VOICE: Otto—he was treasurer—Otto—

VOICE: Otto—died.

VOICE: Gustav was on the shop committee—Gustav—

VOICE: Forced labor in Poland. Typhus.

NARRATOR: That's the way it is in your country, Adolf

—and in the countries you've conquered. And that's the way it isn't going to be here.

Eleven million union men are against you, Adolf. Day shift or night shift or middle shift—they're against you and they're out to get you. And that doesn't just go for the unions. It goes for all labor.

Let me tell you just one little story, Adolf—when Chrysler built its first tank plant. You don't get balmy weather in Michigan, in the winter. But the guys on the job gave up holidays and weekends to stand in slush knee-deep, pouring 51,000 tons of concrete. It snowed and they blew on their fingers and put up 6,500 tons of steel in 70 days. And that was a year before Pearl Harbor. Well, what do you suppose those guys are doing now—picking buttercups?

They did it for overtime pay? Well, let's see your Labor Front match it. And, confidentially, Adolf—it wasn't all for the overtime.

THE FAT AMERICAN VOICE [*breaking in*]: Distressing—racketeers—labor czars—corruption—intimidation—horrible—awful—distressing—scandalous—

NARRATOR: Yeah. We hear *you,* too. We hear the divisive voices. We hear the voices of those who would set class against class, whites against Negroes, Christians against Jews. And we know they're playing Adolf's game—and we're onto them. We hear the voices of those—not many but a few—who would rather beat Labor than Hitler, rather muscle in on Labor than save the United States. And our answer to them and you is:—

[*Loud and derisive Bronx cheer from many voices*]

NARRATOR: Yep, that's coarse. Is isn't refined. I guess we're not very refined when we get mad, Adolf. And you're getting us madder every day.

The worse you make it—the madder we'll get. We know
about the guys on those tankers you've been sinking
—they were working guys like us. We know about
the guys who died on Bataan—a lot of them used to
be working guys like us. There's a cap floating out
on the Atlantic with a union button on it. There's
a kid who was a smart mechanic, but he won't come
back for his tool kit since the Japanese sniper got
him. Well, they were us—and we're them. We don't
need any fancy slogans to keep turning on the heat.
Sure, we're keeping the right to strike. Tell your workers
that—if you dare! Tell them the figures, too—in
May there were a hundred and thirty-seven thousand
man-days lost by strikes. A hundred and thirty-seven
thousand man-days lost. But two hundred and forty-
two million man-days worked. The total loss was just
six one hundredths of one per cent. And let them
think that one over—and you d better think it over,
too.
There's no cockeyed Labor Front in this country. There's
no Gestapo pushing us around. We've adjourned
the big strikes for the duration. We're doing that
freely. We're giving up extras and working overtime. We're doing that freely. We're back of the
President and back of the government. And we're
sending you a letter twenty million workers long.
It's written in steel and flame—in the planes that
fly the oceans and the bombs that drop from the
planes—in the ships that slide down the ways and the
plants that work night and day, day and night. It's
written in brains and muscles and skilled hands
moving fast on the assembly line—in war bonds and
war stamps and the sweat and grind of the shift. It's

written in plain American and it's signed "Yours to blow you sky high—American labor!"

How about it, Assembly Line?

A VOICE: Sending it on to Adolf.

A QUIET VOICE: The time's short.

NARRATOR: How about it, Production, Maintenance, Metal Bench, Center Wings?

VOICE: Sending it on to Adolf!

A QUIET VOICE: The time's passing.

NARRATOR: How about it, twenty million workmen?

VOICES: SENDING IT ON TO ADOLF! SENDING IT ON!

[*Music up*]

(CURTAIN)

4. LETTER FROM A HOUSEWIFE AND MOTHER

HOUSEWIFE: It hasn't come to us yet, the bomb by night,
The machine-gun bullet by day, the shattered house,
The dead child held in the arms for so brief a space,
The other child not found, never found at all,
In spite of the rescue squads and all the cars.
And the people who tried to find him. No, not yet.
I am writing you a letter, Adolf Hitler,
And I'm not saying "Dear Adolf." Being a woman
I can't say that, not even in scorn or jest,
For you are the enemy of all I know,
Of all I feel with my body, know with my mind,
The enemy of all women, everywhere,
And so I can't say "Dear Adolf." Maybe men can
Say that, but I have my own things to say.

I am young and old, middle-aged, with my children grown,
With my children still in my care. I live in a town,
A city, a suburb, a pleasant, tree-shaded street,
A bare street, hard with traffic, ugly with noise,
And the bomb has not reached me yet.
I go up and down
On my day's small business that never begins or stops
Because a family never begins or stops,
It keeps on being a family, every day.
—The leftover steak and the socks and the school reports,
The child with a temperature and the watch at night,
The new kind of salad where Tom will say "What's this?"
But I'll give him waffles, too, and so he won't mind.
        Yes, that's it. That's me,
The millions of us, all over America
Who tell the census-clerk "Occupation—housewife."
And we buy the food for the nation and guard its children,
We keep the house and see that Mister gets fed.
—And because of those things, we hate you, Adolf Hitler.
You are our enemy for life and death.
I do not say it is just or right to hate.
I say we hate you for having caused this hate.
And hate and love are lasting things for a woman.
The selfish and pampered woman of America,
According to your book, say this to you.

WOMAN'S VOICE: We would welcome more demands on
our time, more sacrifices, more jobs to do. My husband
has drilled with the State Guard all year. I teach First Aid
eight hours a week. If we have suffering, we'll manage. We
can take it.

NARRATOR: The thoughtless and idle women of America,
According to your book, say this to you.

WOMAN'S VOICE: I wouldn't have believed that, resilient

as we are, we could have changed drastically in six months. It isn't just the rationing, it cuts deeper.

NARRATOR: The peaceful and flabby women of America, According to your book, say this to you.

WOMAN's VOICE: I always thought war was the worst thing that could happen. I still hate war but I realize that there are things that are worse. We are not a people who could survive by nonresistance. We must fight for our ideals and go on fighting to the end.

NARRATOR: They say—

WOMAN's VOICE: Twice in my lifetime! My husband had to go to war in 1917. Now, thanks to you, he must go again. And this time, my sons too must go. Twice in my life you and people like you have put all I hold dear in danger. I know the price you are making me pay. Our way of life is worth it. But if you know anything about mothers, you will know that I and all other American mothers will see to it that none of us ever pay it again.

NAZI VOICE [*breaking in*]: Say? Well, that's all very fine. But what do they do?

GIRL: Air-raid warden—Post Seven. On duty. All quiet tonight!

NARRATOR: All quiet tonight, but there are thousands like her and, day or night, they're on duty. There are others on other duty—women with children . . .

BOY's VOICE [*amused*]: Gee, what do you know? Mom signed up to be an airplane spotter. Say, when Mom's up in the tower, we'd better all run for the shelters!

WOMAN's VOICE: Yes, that's what he said, at first. But I have good eyes and, after I'd been in the tower for a couple of nights, I discovered he was rather proud of me.

NARRATOR: Just a housewife. 47. In California. But she has good eyes. And here—

GIRL'S VOICE: That makes twelve dozen, Mrs. Carey. All checked and inspected. Now, how about those sweaters?

NARRATOR: Bundles for Britain—Bundles for America—Russian Relief—China Relief—Red Cross—All the thousand things—the thousand things the hands of women can do—

WOMAN'S VOICE: I am now going to demonstrate the triangular bandage for serious head injuries. Please look at the board.

2ND WOMAN'S VOICE: When you pass your training and start working in the hospital, your duties will be necessary rather than glamorous. You will be expected to relieve the regular nurses of a certain amount of detail and routine work which—

NARRATOR: First aid—nurses' aid,
And we've all seen the cartoons
And the jokes about traction splints.
Because here, somehow, we can make fun of ourselves
And yet keep on with the job and get it done.
And then, of course, for all of us, there is this.

CHILD'S VOICE: And, if we were really bombed, I'm to take care of Elly, aren't I, mother? Because she's pretty little.

MOTHER: Yes, dear.

CHILD: And you'll be with us, if you're here—and I remember about the sand in the pails. But if it's in school or anything, I'm not going to be afraid and I'm not going to cause a—an unnecessary disturbance—and neither must Elly—

MOTHER: No, dear. But Elly understands.

CHILD: And remember about lying flat, Elly, if it comes very near and—

[*Music up and down*]

NARRATOR: That's why we hate you.
That's why we can't rest or have peace till you're blacked
          out.
Till you and all who are like you are blacked out
From the world we wish to have born.
You have stretched your hands at our children.
And there is blood on your hands.
The last war was bad and yet it was far away
For us, for most here, for the lucky.
This is near and near and near.
It walks into our own houses, every day,
In blackouts, in the identification discs
Strung 'round the necks of our children.
And we know what those are for.
In the sharp clear voices over the radio
And the going away of men
          This is our war,
Our war, not only our men's, and we mean to fight it,
As you shall see, Adolf Hitler.
I'm not talking now of the women in uniform,
The girls in the plants, the nurses with the Army,
The women pilots, ferrying the big planes,
The pretty girls with curled hair and efficient voices
Who wait in the secret center and train and wait
Who mark the planes on the map-squares and train and
          wait.
We know who they are. We know what they can do
We've had them here from the first.
Women who went with the armies, like Clara Barton,
Women of wilderness-trails, like Rebecca Boone,
Builders of homes on the prairies, like Sarah Lincoln.
—But this is all of us, here.
And the tale is mixed and the equal rights took long,

But from Plymouth Rock, the women went with the men,
And not as toys or chattels. They worked and shared,
They knew who took the brunt of the pioneering,
The women who bore their children on clipper ships,
The women who kept the half-faced camps in the cold,
And they were free women and their strain is in us
And shall go on.

  NEGRO VOICE: Free women? What of me?
What of my millions and my ancient wrong?
What of my people, bowed in darkness still?

  NARRATOR: Dark sister, your wrong is old
And true and grievous and heavy on the heart,
And yet Sojourner Truth could rise and speak,
A woman and a slave,
Speak and be heard, even in darkest days.

  NEGRO VOICE: They are still dark for many of my
   people.
I love my land as well as any of you.
I know that those we war against today
Despise my people and would drive them back
To the old slavery of whips and chains,
The lash upon the back, the ancient wrong.
And yet, even today, we find no place
Even in war, for much that we could do
And would do for—our country.

  NARRATOR: That is true. And yet there is a change.
It comes how slowly but it comes at last,
It comes by inches, yet the ground is won
—And only on free soil, for only there
Can there be growth in change, can there be men
And women, who stand up for others' rights
Not only for their own, who will spend days,
Years, lives in striking at some ancient wrong,

Some old intrenched injustice till it falls.
Sojourner Truth and Susan Anthony,
Jane Addams, Harriet Tubman, Clara Barton,
Women who fought for women—and for men—
For all the people, for the common people,
And each a handful of American dust,
Those are our women!

NAZI VOICE: Yes, that is just the trouble with your corrupt democratic state. Your women mix into all sorts of things that are none of their business. We have put our women in their proper place—bed, cooking, work, children, bed. They don't have to bother their heads about anything else. They are very happy.

NARRATOR: Are you so sure?

NAZI VOICE: We have the record. This is our kind of woman.

NAZI [*woman's voice*]: I am bearing my child for the Fuehrer. I am happy beyond words to bear my child for the Fuehrer. When he grows to manhood he will be a soldier for the Fuehrer. I will be his mother and see him die for the Fuehrer. That is the highest duty of womanhood, to bear children who can fight for the Fuehrer, kill for the Fuehrer, die for the Fuehrer!

WOMAN [*older German*]: They will not let me put my son's death notice in the papers. They say there are too many death notices in the papers. It makes a bad impression.

NAZI [*woman's voice*]: Breed for the Fuehrer!

WOMAN 2 [*German*]: My son got the Iron Cross. They have sent it back to me in a box. They have not sent back my son.

NAZI [*woman's voice*]: Kill for the Fuehrer!

WOMAN 3 [*German*]: There has been another great victory they tell me. Another great victory.

But there is no bread in my house. There are no children
    in my house.

NAZI [*woman's voice*]: Die for the Fuehrer!

VOICES: [*in mechanical obedience, in a long defeated
sigh*]: Sieg—heil—sieg—heil—

NARRATOR: Yes, that's it. That's what you've done.
That's what you've done to the women of Germany.
That's what you've done to their children.
That's what you would do to ours.
To the flesh of our flesh, the bodies of our bodies,
Young, looking up with big eyes—

AN OFFICIAL VOICE: The infant mortality rate in occupied Greece is tragically high and rising.
The Greek babies get no milk. No milk.

NARRATOR: Or the children, gawky and tall,
Gawky as colts and growing out of their clothes,
Just growing up into life—

OFFICIAL VOICE: There are no mortality statistics for
occupied Poland. We cannot compute mortality statistics
for occupied Poland. But we fear that an entire generation
of Polish youth is being wiped out.

NARRATOR: That is your war, that is your kind of war,
The war against the children.
The war against the children of your foes
With bombs and treachery and slow starvation.
The war against the children of your land
To make them shouting slaves of a machine.
And that is why we hate you, Adolf Hitler,
And ask for sacrifice and pray for courage
And will give up whatever must be given,
The pleasant days, the easy luxuries,
Just so your hands will not destroy our children,
Just so your hate will not destroy their hearts.

Oh, yes, we hear the small, divisive voices,
The petty voices, nagging in our ears,
Playing your game.

WOMAN'S VOICE: Well, my dear, of course it all sounds very nice—United Nations. But if you think Britain and Russia won't let us down the minute they get a chance—

MAN'S VOICE: A pint of milk a day for every child in the world! Say that's the silliest idea I ever heard of! Suppose they'll want to give it to the Eskimos, too!

NARRATOR: Yes, those are voices playing your old game—
Class against class, ally against ally,
Race against race, smugness against the dream,
A pint of milk a day for every child?
That's a big order—but it isn't silly.
It isn't silly to women.
We happen to know children and know milk,
We're practical about real things like those,
We're practical in wanting—not just peace
But peace that will mean something.
We're practical in wanting a new world.
Where every kind of child has room to grow.
And, this time—statesmen, premiers, diplomats,
Men of good will and—men of less good will—
Our voices shall be heard at the peace table,
The voices of the free women of the world,
Loud in your ears, persistent as the sea,
"No peace unless it is a peace of justice!
No peace that does not set the children free!"

(CURTAIN)

5. LETTER FROM AN AMERICAN SOLDIER

NARRATOR: Dear Adolf—this is me—one American soldier.

My dog-tag number's in the millions—my draft number came out of the hat in every state in the Union.

I'm from Janesville and Little Rock, Monroe City and Nashua. I'm from Blue Eye, Missouri, and the sidewalks of New York. I'm from the Green Mountains and the big sky-hooting plains, from the roll of the prairie and the rocks of Marblehead, from the little towns where a dog can go to sleep in the middle of Main Street, and the nickel-plated suburbs and the cities that stick their skyscrapers into the sky.

I used to be a carpenter and a schoolteacher and a soda jerker and a mechanic.

I used to be a hackie and a farm hand and a leg-man and a bookkeeper—the son of a guy with money and the son of a guy with none. But I'm a soldier, now.

Four and a half million of us by the end of this year.
Listen to the roll call!

SERGEANT: Adamoffsky, Adams, Anderson, Bailey, Bratillo, Brown—

NARRATOR: That's my outfit—that's us. The biggest
and best-trained army ever raised on American soil.

Ski troops and parachute troops, motorized and mechanized, tank troops and tank destroyers, cooks and cryptographers, bakers and bombardiers—

SERGEANT: —Cohen, Costello, Daughterty, Di Rosa,
Dupont—

NARRATOR: From Alaska to Australia—from Australia
to Ulster—in the cold skies and the hot—under desert suns
and clear skies and jungle rains—

That's us—the United States Army!

[*Music up and down*]

NARRATOR: And we're not writing letters, Adolf. We're
on the job.

We weren't picked out for our looks or our Aryan names.

We weren't picked out to heil heels or to chew up small
countries that never did us any harm.

We weren't picked out to sit around on our parking spaces
and wait for you to be nasty.

We've been picked out for a job and a very large and extensive job and we mean to police it up.

And that means you and Musso and old man Hiro-Stab-in-the-Back and all the rest of you rug-biters.

Sure, we let you get away with a lot. We sat around and
argued, over here, while you were cooking with gas.
But that's all over.

Let me tell you a few things about us—about the kind of
army we are. They won't make you happy.

When my bunch went in, we had a drill corporal from

upstate Georgia. He didn't read the papers much—
he'd rather go to town and pick a scrap with the
MPs. But he drilled us well—"hut, two, three, four"
—and every day he kept saying—

VOICE: "Now you birds damn well pay attention here.
This business is for keeps."

NARRATOR: That was March, 1941. But he knew what
was coming. And we listened but—well, most of us had
left good jobs and that seemed pretty important. We had
a bunch of Italians and they missed their spaghetti and con-
versation. We had a bunch of Maine lads and they sweated
under the Georgia sun and thought about the lakes beginning to melt, back in Maine. We had some Poles—and they
knew the score. Their folks had heard from Warsaw. But
they didn't argue much. They just kept humping.

Sure—that was what we were like—just a little while ago.
We beefed. And we wondered why we were in the Army.

But we learned how to handle guns and we learned about
Army chow. We learned what a march under pack
means, and we learned about teamplay and discipline. We got confidence in our weapons and pride
in a well-oiled unit.

Yes, it was all pretty new. But when most of my company,
at the end of thirteen weeks, marched off to join a
new division—well, some of them were bawling like
kids. Because, somehow, without lectures and orders
and editorials, there had jelled a sense of comrade-
ship that would make your well-advertised Gemein-
schaftgeist look sick.

And then we trained some more—and waited. For the answer you gave us—you and your Axis pals. And that
was when civilians worried about our morale. Because military service wasn't our chosen way of life.

We wanted to get a job done and get through with it. And maneuvering against a Blue Army (which we knew was Yanks all the time) didn't seem to be settling much. Even if it was making the U.S. Army a good one, as you'll soon find out.

So that Sunday, when we lay on our bunks, full of chicken and black-eyed peas, and idly turned on the radio—and got the news—we didn't have to count pulses to know what our morale was. It was there. Because now the real job was starting and that meant something. "It's about time," one soldier said.

And that's about all you need to know about us, Adolf. Period.

SERGEANT: —Dalton, Davis, Dombrowski, Ettelsohn, Edwards, Farrar—

NARRATOR: Like to hear from some of them? Here's one. From Ohio. Used to drive a bus. Now he's mechanized infantry.

VOICE: In the part of Ohio I come from, lots of people have religious convictions against war. I keep these prayers at the back of my mind every day and believe these prayers. I pray for peace. But I am not so much like those people in Ohio as I used to be. My convictions are that war is evil and that the evil men are those who started it. When you ask me what I have personally to be angry against the Nazis and the Japs, that is my answer. They have hurt me and my people by making us fight a war that in our religion is bad. I don't know if I have made myself clear but Hitler is my personal enemy and I aim to stop him.

NARRATOR: And—prayers don't make a soldier, Adolf? Not by your book? Well—ask about Lee's army—the Army of Northern Virginia. They prayed when they felt like it. Here's another.

VOICE: I have always made my living in this country. Now I must fight for it. This country didn't ask for war. I know I didn't. But now we are going to win. The least thing I am fighting for is to get my job back. And it was a good job, worth fighting for.

NARRATOR: That was a twenty-six-year-old garment worker—sorry—corporal in the Air Force. And here's a marine—just back from the Atlantic Patrol—and sore. Sore because he's been made an instructor and isn't with his outfit.

VOICE: All I want to be is where I belong, in a mortar platoon of the Marines. Don't get me wrong. I'm not trying to wave the flag or become "Joe Hero." But, surely, patriotism is something more than knowing the words of "The Star-Spangled Banner." I'll admit that, ten years hence, nobody may give a damn about what the boys in uniform did today. Those who die in action will be hardly a memory and those who come back maimed will be an expense, a bore and a nuisance. But, for today, let's not forget the foxholes of Bataan or the rape of Nanking or the ghettoes of Poland or the million and one other acts that violate every human and decent instinct of man.

I've seen death many times recently and dodged it on several occasions, and, if I get killed—what the hell. Nobody ever left this world alive and very few of us get to die for a cause. If I do get through, I will have had the satisfaction of knowing that I did try to do a man's job.

NARRATOR: And here's a letter from Bataan—February 12, 1942.

VOICE: "Dear Mother and Dad and Frances: This letter may never be delivered. It will go to Corregidor and there await transportation.

I am proud to be part of the fight that is being made here.
Bataan may fall but the eventual outcome of the war
is foreordained.

I have seen some horrible things happen and had my share
of narrow escapes. But I have also seen some very
wonderful acts of courage, self-sacrifice and loyalty.
At last I have found what I have searched for all my
life—a cause and a job in which I can lose myself
completely.

Life and my family have been very good to me and given
me everything I have really wanted. Should anything
happen to me here, it will not be like closing a book
in the middle. In the last two months I have done a
lifetime of living and been part of one of the most
unselfish, cooperative efforts that has ever been made.

Mistakes may have been made—but that has nothing to do
with the manner in which my comrades on Bataan—
both Filipino and American have reacted to their
trial of fire. If the same selfless spirit were devoted to
world betterment in time of peace, what a good world
we would have (and "how dull" I can hear the
younger generation muttering).

This letter is written to send you all my love and thanks
for just being my family. It is written with no so-
called premonitions. My chances are pretty good. So
I'll send it on its way. Keep 'em flying—West!

Your loving son and brother."

NARRATOR: No—we haven't heard from that lieutenant.
Not since Corregidor fell. But—we'll keep 'em flying.

We're not talking about being Joe Hero. There's a long,
dirty, bloody job ahead of us. We know that.

Wars mean filth and thirst and pain and the scream of the
dive bombers on top of you and going on to the end

of endurance, and beyond. Wars mean seeing your best friend killed beside you and it's only afterwards you have time to think about him, because the line must be held. All right, mister, you started it rolling. We know the score.

We're the guys who take cars apart and put them together, just for fun. We're the guys who fiddle with radio sets and are crazy about the comics—Bat Man and Terry and the Pirates and Donald Duck and all kinds of people who do things they aren't supposed to do. The Army wasn't supposed to get away with bombing Tokyo. But it did. The Navy wasn't supposed to sink five Jap aircraft carriers in the battle of Midway. But it did.

We don't build armies just to put guys in uniform and shove civilians around. We build them to fight and win battles. We build them just the same way we built Boulder Dam—and out of the same kind of stuff.

No, we weren't so much on slogans, Adolf. We aren't talking about a new order or a co-prosperity sphere. We aren't even talking much yet about a new world. And when it's over and the bands start playing—they're just as likely to play "Don't Sit Under the Apple-tree" as they are "The Star-Spangled Banner." Because we're that way.

We kid about things that mean a lot to us. We make wise-cracks about generals and presidents. We say "Don't give us the oil" when we mean business. And we mean business now.

And, back of us, all the time, there's a roll call and a knowl-edge—

SERGEANT: —Follett, Fraser, Garrett, Hamilton, Herkimer—

NARRATOR: That's the muster roll of the Revolution, Adolf—the muster roll of free men who fought for their country because she had to be born. And they got worse chow than ours and they got paid off in paper—and, if they were living, afterwards they went back to their farms and hoed corn. But they knew what they'd done. And they were satisfied.

SERGEANT: —Izard, Jones, Jacobson, Jackson, Kearney, Lee Fitzhugh, Lee, R. E.—

NARRATOR: That's the roll of the Civil War, Adolf. And, out of it, the Union lived and the free thing went ahead. It cost blood and toil and long bitterness but it made us one nation.

SERGEANT: —Levinsky, Liebowitz, Liggett, MacArthur, McCook, Maginetti—

NARRATOR: That's the last war, Adolf—the Rainbow Division and the First Division and all the divisions—the two million who went to France. And we came in late and we had to borrow other folks equipment because ours wasn't ready. But the record's written from Cantigny to the Argonne. This time we'll have the equipment—our factories are turning it out. And this time we aren't going to stop with just "saving democracy"—and then running out on it. This time we're after a durable peace—and it isn't your kind.

SERGEANT: —Nason, Nathan, Nininger, O'Brien, O'Hare, Orlando—

NARRATOR: That's a few of the new names, Adolf. No, the roll isn't finished. It won't be finished till you are.

SERGEANT: —Papagos, Patterson, Prokosch, Pryor, Quintanilla, Quisada, Que Lung—

NARRATOR: Chinese, Italian, Greek, Bohemian, British, Mexican—the sons of the men who fought six wars and won them—the sons of the men who came here to get away from wars. But they're all Americans now, Adolf—and all against you. Against you and the Nipponese pals you sicked on us at Pearl Harbor—against you and all your ideas and ways. We don't like being ordered around, though we'll take it and like it in wartime. We think one man's as good as the next and maybe better. If we feel like going to church, we'll go to the church we pick out and the next guy can go to his. If we want to get married, we'll marry the girl we like—and the guy who makes a crack about her ancestry had better look out for his teeth. If we don't like the people who run our government, we'll change them by peaceable election. That's us. That's our platform. And behind us are a hundred and thirty million Americans.

SERGEANT: —Raconski, Rattray, Rourke, Saltonstall, Socepanowics—

NARRATOR: All the funny names there are—yes, Adolf—the old names and the new—the names that made America from Jamestown to the Cherokee Strip and back and forth and across and up and down. Only this time, the building will be bigger than anything we've ever tried. This time the roll call will not end with the armistice.

SERGEANT: —Camacho, Chiang Kai-shek, Churchill, Cripps, Curtin, De Gaulle, Litvinoff, Quezon, Roosevelt, Stalin, Van Mook, Wallace, Willkie—

NARRATOR: Yes—this time—it's for a new world. But not for yet. Now it's the march in the mud and the heat on the steel box of the tank and the stutter of the tail gun from the bombing plane. And yet—

SERGEANT: The command is forward.

NARRATOR: Now—it's fever and wounds and the stink of the slit trench. And yet—

SERGEANT: The command is forward.

NARRATOR: The command is forward. March!

[*Music up and down*]

NARRATOR: Got a nice rug to chew on, Adolf? Vanilla or chocolate? Well, make it a double one with maraschino. You'll need it before we're through.

(CURTAIN)

6. LETTER FROM A FOREIGN BORN AMERICAN

NARRATOR: Adolf Hitler! Reichschancellor! Reichs-
leader! Reichsdestroyer! You will know my voice. It is the
voice of the peoples you have crushed and starved and shot
—the voice of the peoples of Europe, held down but unsub-
dued. The voice of suffering peoples, tricked into war on
your side by their bad and stupid rulers. The voice of suffering peoples, beaten down by your armies—but waiting,
waiting, waiting in terrible patience for the dawn and the
liberation and the end of you and your kind. It is under-
ground, that voice, in Europe. It burrows like a mole under-
ground—it whispers like the night wind through the air. It
does not speak loudly—yet. But when it speaks, your hang-
man dies. But my voice comes from America, not from
Europe. I speak to you—I speak to my fellow Americans.
I speak for the alien-born. I speak for many stocks and

many mother tongues. I speak for old famous cities and
peasant villages—for the lands where custom is old, where
the fields have been tilled for many generations—the lands
of our mothers' milk and our fathers' endeavor. And I speak
for the men and women who left these behind to come
here. We came here to this country as children—we came
here a few short years ago. We came with no English at all
—with a few words picked up somehow—with the painful,
scholarly phrases you learn in books and the scraps of old-
fashioned slang we were so proud of knowing. We came in
the different clothes, with the different haircuts, homesick
and excited and weary and looking forward and wondering.
Wondering if it was true—if it could be true. If America
was what they said—if we would be welcomed or hated,
given a place or despised. For roots are hard to tear up,
even for bread or freedom. The heart looks back for a
while, even when the body has crossed an ocean. Was it true
what they said—that this was a land where your stock or
your birthplace or your name did not matter beside what
you were and what you could do? Was it true we'd have
rights like the rest and a chance like the rest? Was it true
we could be Americans? Hear my friend from the Lebanon.

ARMENIAN VOICE: In my village in the Lebanon, when
I was a boy, when the governor's carriage passed down the
street, everyone jumped up and saluted. If you didn't salute
—well, then you were due for trouble. Ours was a subject
country and when our village elders found themselves oppressed, they would raise helpless hands and say "It is your
governor and your God." And there was no appeal from
God or the governor. So, when I came here, at twenty, with
others of my compatriots, we knew little of many things.
We had heard the United States was a land of plenty and
liberty. Well, that sounded all right—but, to our minds,

the plenty came first. For the rest of it—well, there would doubtless be governors here just like our governors. So a man examined my papers, at the port of Boston, and I stood before him, shaking in my boots. He was an official—a governor. But when he had finished with my papers he got up and shook me by the hand. He wished me good luck in my new country. I have never forgotten that. I will never forget it. What did we find here? Other helping hands were stretched out to us. We found that neither race nor birth nor faith stood in the way of our advancement—our becoming men among men. We found a land willing and ready to adopt us and give us the rights and privileges of its natural sons—a land that taught us the meaning of liberty and made of us freemen. Now, we have no other home and no other cause. Those who have always been rich do not always know the value of a treasure as well as those who once were poor. Those who have never thirsted do not know how sweet water can be. But we, who were poor in liberty and thirsty for free air, know what we have found here. The least we can do, now this land and its way of life is threatened as never before, is to pledge our lives, our fortunes, and our sacred honor to its cause.

NARRATOR: Hear my friend who was born in Hungary.

HUNGARIAN: America is my country and America is the home of my children and will be the home of their children. My eldest daughter is in love with an Irish fellow and she told me she dreams about him in English. This surely is my country when my daughter loves an Irish fellow and dreams about him in English and she speaks to me about him in Hungarian. I know how to read but my wife never learned how, but we both know we don't have to lick the boots of our bosses and when my daughter's fellow—he's in the Army—when he writes her a letter it makes us all happy. What can Hitler do to make us happy? He's the devil's own friend and we almost feel sorry for the devil because he has Hitler's friendship. What else can I tell you? I'm a citizen—I can vote—I never could do that in the old country. And I go to church and there are no spies looking at me and I can speak to God and I don't have to mind Hitler. The wife and I pray for America. We ask God to help us in this war and we pray for the old country's happiness, too—to rid it from the Nazis—and we pray for the village where we were born and hope that someday it will be free. And we buy war bonds every month—America must win. She will win!

NARRATOR: Hear my friend from the Germany you slew.

GERMAN: I fight you because you taught me the full meaning of a verse by the poet Schiller "es kann der Froemmste nicht in Frieden leben, wenn es dem boesen Nachbar nicht gefaellt"—A saint cannot live in peace if his wicked neighbor does not like it. I was a pacifist once—an intellectual—a thinker. You drove me out of Germany—I took refuge in France. For the first time, there, I began to know what freedom is. Then you invaded France. I took part in that terrible retreat—I know what you did there. I do not want to talk about that, but I know what you did. In the end, by great luck, I was rescued and came to the U.S.A. And there I saw what amazed me—an organized democracy, defending its freedoms. Hitler, you will never understand what America means to us. It does not only mean the last refuge of freedom. It is a society in which a man may have his way and stand for his own interests and ideas, but which does not give its enemies a chance to overthrow it. It is a society rich enough not to fear need and strong enough not to fear anything. It gives freedom to all nationalities but lets them organize their contributions to the whole. A society where I don't risk my head if I say "Why don't we get this done?"—but am asked to suggest how I think it could be done. You may boast of your ability to keep the appearance that everything is well in Germany. This society here would break down the moment when everybody should say everything is well. It gets things done by criticisms and discussion—by 130,000,000 people criticizing, discussing—and co-operating. And that is why you will never win this war. The American people are fighting for their way of life. They cannot be scared into panic —they will not be brought to their knees by your war of nerves. They become more decided every day your war goes on. They know they have no way but to win it.

NARRATOR: Hear the voices.

VOICE: The only way I could figure America was the sun shining all the time and a bakery shop in the middle of the street.

VOICE: Like you, I once was a corporal, but unlike you, I was fortunate enough to come to the United States in a crowded ship, in steerage. I arrived penniless and friendless but America gave me priceless freedom and opportunity.

VOICE: I had almost forgotten there were places where people still went to the polls and voted for the man they thought would be the best man for the job.

VOICE: I know of my driven people. I know that here I am free.

NARRATOR: These are only a few, Herr Reichschancellor. There are so many, many others. There are the Rumanians of Salem, Ohio, who gathered together last Flag Day, June 14th, and said:

VOICE: It is a great pain to us that the flag of our native country cannot appear alongside the flag of this great country. But we can endure this pain because we know that not the Rumanian flag is in disgrace but the knaves who bowed to Hitler. Friends, bear up! Uncle Sam will fix it, all right.

NARRATOR: And that day they raised fifteen hundred dollars—for an ambulance for Uncle Sam. And there is the Reverend Frank Imery Vass, a pastor, alien-born—whose son went down with the *Lexington* in the battle of the Coral Sea. And he said:

VOICE: We are glad our son fought for America.

NARRATOR: No, I cannot count them all. I cannot summon them all. But I know the feeling in their hearts. You have been deceived about us, Herr Reichschancellor. You have been badly deceived. You have bought a few traitors, here and there. You have planted a few spies. You have caused a few deluded men and women to doubt democracy. You have tried your oldest trick on us, to get us fighting among ourselves—labor against management, Protestant against Catholic, Christian against Jew, native-born against foreign-born. But we—we are the litmus paper and the test of democracy—we the many, the uncounted, the ordinary, who quietly take our pledge to the flag you hate and the freedom you hate and the rights of man that you hate—and who quietly pledge to that flag, of our own free will, not only our bodies but our hearts. No, all is not perfect here, Herr Chancellor. I am a free man, I can tell you the truth and I will. They talk about Hunkies and Dagoes, Micks and Pollacks. They say, "We got too many foreigners." They say, "Well, what can you expect with all these foreigners?" And, every time someone says that, you rub your hands and smile. Well—smile—that is all quite true. I've heard an Italian truck farmer in New England say to his Czech neighbor, "This was a good town before all these dumb foreigners came in." Yes, I've heard that. Make the most of it. But, you see—that's it, Herr Chancellor. Paul Pappas isn't a foreigner because everybody knows Paul Pappas—he runs the candy store. Dr. Tashian isn't a foreigner because everybody knows Dr. Tashian. Foreigners, here, aren't the people you see around. They're the next boatload. In no matter what bad accent I speak, I can say "I am an American" and no one will laugh. These are good American names—Stone, Marshall, Saltonstall, Magruder, Frost. These are good American names—LaGuardia, Eisenhower, Adamic, Knudsen, Nimitz. They are all good American names and, as we say in America, that is all. Period. I cannot explain this to you because there is no way of explaining and your crazy mind cannot understand. I can say that the son of an Italian stonecutter can be lieutenant governor of the State of New York. I can say that a man born in England can be Justice of the U. S. Supreme Court. I can say that a man born in Germany can be a United States senator. And nobody thinks that is queer and nobody says much about it, till the obituaries are written. I can say that those who fight for freedom in the United States Army today have every name in the world. But, still, that is not enough. We are quiet, we alien-born, because, after all, we are still learning. We are even a little shy. When our children come back from school, so assured and yet with questions, we are proud of those children. We see them grow big and free, taking rights for granted. That is fine, that is what we want. But even they do not know the price of freedom as we know it. Not even they. We hear those long in the land who talk of their country—our country. We know who speaks true and who speaks false. And we listen well to those who speak true, for their fathers made this land. But even many of them do not know the price of freedom as we know it. Not even they. We, the Pilgrims of a thousand unnamed and forgotten

Mayflowers—our freedom and our citizenship was bought with all we have. It was bought with a dream in the mind —the dream of a free, lucky country where life would be good and human beings equal. It was bought with travel and poverty and the wrenching up of old memories and fear and hope and faith. With a great price we bought this freedom. And that price seems little, today. We would pay it again, Herr Reichschancellor. Skin for skin, we would pay it. Ten times over we would pay it. There was a town called Lidice, Adolf Hitler. We know what happened to that town. There was a city named Rotterdam and a city named Cracow. There was the house where the family lived and the things they did—the cousins and friends and parents who are dead—the brothers and sisters who starve and survive and fight. And there is the walking around here—just in free air—just the walking around where you buy a paper at the corner and nobody asks who you are. That is why we are against you, Adolf Hitler—we, the alien-born, the new Americans whose children shall be Americans. Against you and against you forever. Against you living or dying, against you waking or sleeping, against you every minute, every hour, every day. You would bring to this country the things we escaped and hated. You would poison the air and the water and the minds of our growing children. You would drag them back—not even to the life we knew—but to the life of the serf, the life of the slave. But we have tasted liberty and soon liberty walks in the streets— No, we were not at Lexington or Gettysburg. But the names that we make today shall be names as shining as those. All over the country they answer—the Americans—the alien-born. All over the country they answer—for the free world —the good thing—the old tradition and the new—

VOICES [*strong but accented*]: I pledge my allegiance to the American flag—

NARRATOR: Those are Greeks, Italians, Croats, Slovenes —Americans!

VOICES [*building*]: —And to the Republic for which it stands—

NARRATOR: Those are Rumanians, Bohemians, Russians, Latvians, Norwegians—Americans!

VOICES: One nation, indivisible, with liberty and justice for all—

NARRATOR: Danes, Swedes, Irish, French, Spaniards— Americans!

[*Voices continue flag-pledge*]

NARRATOR: Fumbling voices—voices with accents— with every accent—but meaning it, meaning every word! We, who are the test of democracy—the litmus paper of democracy—

VOICES: I PLEDGE MY ALLEGIANCE TO THE AMERICAN FLAG!

[*Music way up and down*]

NARRATOR: And that is all, Herr Reichschancellor. That is all. Period.

(CURTAIN)

THANKSGIVING DAY—1941

Broadcast over the NBC Red Network, November 19, 1941.

The script was read by Brian Donlevy, the program was produced and directed by Ned Tollinger, with music directed by Gordon Jenkins.

THANKSGIVING DAY—1941

There are many days in the year that we celebrate, but this one is wholly of our earth. Three hundred and eighteen years ago, long before we were ever a nation, a handful of men and women who wished to live for an idea and were willing to die for it, first set this day apart as a day of thanks. They were neither rich nor powerful, those men and women of Plymouth; they had bought the very ground they stood on by the deaths of their nearest and dearest. After three years of toil and suffering, they had made a small settlement and planted a few cleared fields. Behind them lay the ocean; before them, the untamed forest. They had come a long way to stand between sea and forest; they had left all ease and security behind them. Even so, they could not know whether their experiment in freedom would succeed or fail; they could not even be

71

sure that Plymouth Colony would live through the next winter. It is hard for us to realize that; it was what they faced, under all their courage. Nevertheless, cut off from all they had known, alone beyond our knowledge, they gave thanks in humble sincerity for God's mercies and the gift of corn.

Today, one hundred and thirty million Americans keep the day they first set apart. We all know what Thanksgiving is—it's turkey day and pumpkin pie day—the day of the meeting of friends and the gathering of families. It does not belong to any one creed or stock among us, it does not honor any one great man. It is the whole family's day —the whole people's day—the day at the turn of the year when we can all get together, think over the past months a little, feel a sense of harvest, a kinship with our land. It is one of the most secure and friendly of all our feasts. And yet it was first founded in insecurity, by men who stood up to danger. And that spirit is still alive.

This year it is and must be a sober feast. And yet, if we know our hearts, as a people, we can be grateful—not in vainglory or self-satisfaction, but for essential things. Let us speak out some of the things that are in our hearts.

We are grateful to those before us who made this country and fought for it, who hewed it out of the wilderness and sowed it with the wheat of freedom. We are grateful to all Americans, of all kinds and sorts and beliefs, who stood up on their hind legs and protested against injustice, from the first plantings till now. We are grateful to the great men, present and past, who have risen from our earth to lead us, and to the innumerable many whose names are not in the histories but without whose laughter and courage, endurance and resolution, all our history would have been in vain.

We are grateful for our land itself—not for its material resources or the plenty of its fields—but for its vast diversity under the great bond of union. We are grateful for Connecticut elm and Georgia pine, for the big stars over Texas and the bread of the Middle West. We are grateful to little towns with common place names where people get along with each other, not because they are told to, but just because they believe in getting along. That's the way we like to have it, and mean to have it. We are grateful because we believe that all those who would confuse and divide us with counsels of class hatred, race hatred, despair and defeat know little of the temper of our people. We are grateful to all the others, to every good neighbor, to each man and woman of good will.

We are grateful to those who guard the far-flung outposts of our nation—to the men on the lonely sea patrols, on the high patrols of the air. To the men in the camps, to the men on the ships, to the men of the air, to all those who keep watch and guard, we pay our tribute today. Nor can that tribute be paid in fine words alone. These are our own men we have summoned—it is the business of all of us to back them with the firm resolution of a united nation. And that shall be done.

Most of all we are grateful, under God, for the spirit that walks abroad in this land of ours—the spirit that has made us and kept us free. It is many years indeed since men first came here for freedom. The democracy we cherish is the work of many years and many men. But as those first men and women first gave thanks, in a dark hour, for the corn that meant life to them, so let us give thanks today— not for the little things of the easy years but for the land we cherish, the way of life we honor, and the freedom we shall maintain.

A TIME TO REAP

Broadcast over WABC and the CBS Network, Thursday, November 26, 1942, as a special Thanksgiving night program for the Office of War Information.

The narrator was Henry Hull, the program was produced and directed by Robert Lewis Shayon and the music composed and conducted by Ben Ludlow.

The Honorable Claude R. Wickard, Secretary of Agriculture, took part in the program by reading his own speech.

A TIME TO REAP

NARRATOR [*simply*]: To every thing there is a season—
and a time to every purpose under the heavens—a time to
be born and a time to die—a time to plant—and a time
to reap—

[*Music: Sweep into hymn*]

CHORUS: [*sings*]: Come, ye thankful people, come,
                Raise the song of harvest home:

[*Hums, and under with orchestra*]

[*Music*]

CHORUS [*up*]: Come to God's own temple, come,
                Raise the song of harvest home.

[*Music: Segue and paint under*]

NARRATOR [*quietly and soberly*]: Thanksgiving night.
It's quiet tonight in America. But the great harvest is in.

Follow the westward sun as it sinks in the Pacific—the
great harvest is in. Follow the rising stars as they shine on

Provincetown and Plymouth and the coast where the Pilgrims first landed—the great harvest is in. From the grainlands of the Middle West to the black earth of the Delta, from the cold, first springs of the Connecticut to the valley of the San Joaquin, it is there, abundant, fruitful, the great harvest of our land. It does not belong to one man and no one man made it. It is the American people's— part of their flesh and their bone and their war—the greatest harvest in all our years as a nation. As we sit at table, today, let us remember that.

[*Music*]

NARRATOR: Every man and woman and boy and girl who has worked and labored for this harvest has served our country. Stand up to be counted!

[*Sound: Stand up from chairs*]

NARRATOR: How many?

MAN: Call us six million, round about. Six million farmers. And wives, and children.

NARRATOR: That's a pretty big family. Where are you?

MAN: I'm from Lincoln County, Nebraska.

MAN: I'm from Washington County, Maine.

WOMAN: Deaf Smith County, Texas.

BOY: R. F. D. Number Two. The nearest town's Pretty Prairie.

MAN: Borough of Stonington.

WOMAN: Roanoke.

MAN: Just ask where the tall corn grows. That's where I come from.

MAN: You may raise good crops where you come from. I'm not disputing it. But you can't beat the Cumberland Valley.

WOMAN: Well, how about the Dakotas? How about them?

MAN: If you're talking about dairy-farming—Wisconsin.

MAN: Now, if you've all said your say, I'd just like to say one or two words about California. Our climate—

NARRATOR: Just a minute—just a minute. You're all of you right—of course. There's one sort of industry here and another one there. But there isn't a State in the Union without farms and farmers.

[*Music: Sneak in and stay in—changing with mood*]

NARRATOR: And through war and peace they go on. From the wooden plow to the four-row cultivator—they go on. Men must have food. And it isn't a come-day, go-day, God-send-Sunday job to raise it. It takes all there is of a man.

NEW ENG.AND VOICE: Don't have to tell me about that. First grant of my land was made to Ezra Perkins. Anno Domini 1664—all down in the township records. Well, he'd hardly cleared his land when the Indians came and scalped him. Must have been quite a surprise to him—would be to me. But, we're still using the spring he first picked out— and the land's been farmed ever since. Still stony, but we make out. Takes more than stones and scalpings to root up New England. How about you, neighbor?

MIDWEST VOICE: My folks went out to Kansas for free soil. They went out there in a wagon and they weren't more than well started when the grasshoppers came. They ate every blade in the ground—they ate everything but the clothes off your back, and some say they tried those. But Kansas, well, she's Kansas, and my folks stayed. Got a good farm now—you won't see a better one. No, you can't be licked by a grasshopper. Not in Kansas.

SWEDISH VOICE: I know. It was not easy at first, in Minnesota. It was a beautiful land, but I had to learn the new language and the new ways. But, with years, there comes a harvest not all of the land. My children, they are Americans, and so am I. That is worth a great deal to me.

SOUTHERN VOICE: Well—we've seen good times and hard times down South. We used to grow all cotton, but we're using our land a lot better nowadays. We're raising food and livestock with our cotton and tobacco, and we're doing right well. There's some of that harvest that's mine.

VOICE: And mine . . .

VOICE: And mine . . .

VOICES: And mine.

[*Music: Up and out fast*]

NARRATOR: An old story? Yes, very old. A story of toil and struggle and patient skill—the struggle of human beings with earth and weather, with prairie and stony ground and uncleared forest so that men should have food. A story not always known—not always realized. Though when we first came here, we knew. We knew that men must have food or die in their tracks. The Pilgrims knew it, searching for food in the wilderness in bitter weather.

PILGRIM VOICE [*music*]: This done, we marched to the place where we had the corn formerly and digged and found the rest, of which we were very glad—so we had in all about ten bushels which would serve us for seed. And sure it was God's good providence that we found this corn, for else we know not what we should have done—

NARRATOR: Just ten bushels of seed corn! But it saved the whole Plymouth Colony. And yet—what happened, even so, in 1623? Let William Bradford speak. . . .

[*Music: Sneak in and back*]

BRADFORD: Yet, notwithstanding all their pains and industry and hopes of a large crop, the Lord seemed to blast and take away the same by a great drought and great heat from the third week of May till the middle of July, without any rain. And some of the drier grounds were parched like withered hay. So they set apart a solemn day of humiliation, to seek the Lord by prayer in this great distress. And he was pleased to give them an answer. For all morning it was clear weather and very hot, but toward evening it began to rain, without wind or thunder or violence, which did so revive the corn as was wonderful to see. And afterwards the Lord sent them such seasonable showers interchanged with fair warm weather as caused them a fruitful harvest. For which mercy, in time convenient, they set apart a day of Thanksgiving.

[*Music: Up and continue under*]

NARRATOR: The first Thanksgiving, after the drought and the rain. Nor was it a feast of plenty—not as we think it. The crumbs of our plenty would have been great wealth to the Pilgrims. But, it was a feast of purpose—a feast of the resolute, who had come through drought and starvation and thanked God. And that purpose went on through the years. The good land—the fertile land drew men and women from every country in Europe to live here in peace, like neighbors.

[*Music: Change to Yankee Doodle*]

NARRATOR: And yet, when there was a war and a revolution—

VOICE SINGING [*accompanied by fife and drum*]: Yankee Doodle came to town,
Riding on a pony,
He stuck a feather in his hat
And called him macaroni.

MALE CHORUS: Yankee Doodle, keep it up,
Yankee Doodle Dandy—
Mind the music and the step—[*fade*]

And with the girls be handy.

NARRATOR: Of course, we all know it. But, who was Yankee Doodle? Why, he was a farmer's boy—you can tell that from the song. He rode into town on a farm pony. And the Yankee farmers took that jumpy little song—and their muskets—and shot their way to independence and freedom. But—it didn't always go so well for Yankee Doodle. Not always, through the Revolution. Time after time, a farmer named George Washington had to say . . .

WASHINGTON: I must represent once more to the Congress the hard condition of my men. Once more they are without rations, except such as may be furnished by a few friendly farmers and these supplies are almost at an end.

A MASSACHUSETTS VOICE: A handful of weevily wheat! A man can't fight on that! I'm as strong for the cause of Liberty as any man. But I'm giving up this musket and going home.

A VIRGINIA VOICE: You said that three weeks running, Massachusetts. But you ain't made tracks for home yet.

MASSACHUSETTS VOICE: Well, this time I mean it, Virginia. A man can't fight on with an empty belly forever!

VIRGINIA VOICE: You and I kin. We've done it before. But I wish the home folks could know what it's like to fight starvation as well as the soldiers. I just wish they could know—what it's like—

[*Music: Short set and under*]

NARRATOR: Not so pretty, is it? But it happened. Men need food—and Washington's men starved and sickened at Valley Forge without it. Fighting men need food—and in Lee's heroic Army of Northern Virginia, there were men who would fight for a while and then go home for a while to raise a crop. They had to. But—it wasn't a good system and it can't be done today. You can't have part-time soldiers and part-time farmers. You can't let your fighting men go hungry. A nation at war today must produce not only the guns and the planes but the food that will win that war. Food is powder and shot. [*Music out*] We've been hearing about our great harvest. Let's see where it goes. Let's go to an embarkation point for a minute. They're loading a convoy.

[*Sound: Dock noises, rattle of cranes, etc.*]

NARRATOR: We'll go on board and ask a few questions. Excuse me, mister,—could you tell me what's in this case?

VOICE: Orange-juice concentrate. For the American Air Force. Hard to get oranges now in a lot of the places they fly. But we ship 'em the concentrate and they say it's O. K.

NARRATOR: What about this one?

VOICE: Dried eggs. For Britain. They need 'em. You know how they're rationed in Britain—you know what their army's doing in Libya.

NARRATOR: And this?

VOICE: Dried milk. Destination—well, I'll let you guess on that one. Might end up in Greece, feeding hungry little children. Might end up in North Africa with the AEF. Might end up almost anywhere. But wherever it ends up, it'll help our side.

NARRATOR: North Africa—Britain—the Solomons—Australia—Russia—Alaska—China—India—say, this sounds like a pretty big job.

VOICE: You bet it's a big job. You a farmer?

NARRATOR: Well—I know some farmers.

VOICE: Well, you go back and tell them that this is about the biggest job any farmer's ever tackled. They aren't farming their own farms any more—they're farming the seas and the skies and the deserts and the foreign lands. And if they could stand where I stand and see what happens to all the things they raise—and where it goes—they'd know the job they're doing and so would the rest of the nation.

[*Music: Punctuate and under*]

NARRATOR: Yes, we know the job our farmers are doing. Food isn't just food in this war. It's a weapon, one of our biggest, and if anybody thinks the farmer isn't a fighter— well, let's see—

[*Music: Segue Army mess call*]

NARRATOR: That's the Army mess call. Mess call for our six and a quarter million men in United States uniform all over the world. And each American soldier eats a ton of food a year. They must have food. All men on duty, afloat or ashore—over six million and a quarter men. They must have food.

[*Sound: Factory whistle*]

NARRATOR: That's a factory shift going on at a munitions plant. The men who make the shells and the guns and the planes. Twenty million workers. And they must have food.

[*Sound: Shuffle of feet—faint, unrecognizable voices*]

NARRATOR: And those—those are hungry children. The children of the occupied countries we mean to free and are freeing. The children and the women and the strong men, worn down by years of hunger, dragging listless feet toward death. And then—someday—sometime—

CHILDREN'S VOICES: The bread! The food! The good food! If you please—if you please—

CHILD'S VOICE: My sister first—she is so very hungry—

VOICE: Milk. I have heard about milk. Is it real? Is it true?

FARM VOICE: Well, all right, kids—pitch in. Plenty more

where it came from. We're Americans. We don't like people to starve.

[*Music: Sneak in*]

VOICES: Americans! The Americans! Bread! Food! Freedom!

[*Music: Up and tag*]

NARRATOR: Bread. Food. Freedom. They're pretty good words for Thanksgiving Day. They're pretty good weapons too.

AMERICAN WOMAN'S VOICE [*angry*]: Well, it all sounds very pretty, I'm sure. But what about me? Why, I had to go to four stores—actually four stores—before I could get my favorite brand of coffee. And my butcher was all out of French lamp chops. It's disgraceful!

NARRATOR [*chuckling*]: Lady, coffee is one of the few things we don't raise ourselves . . . and it takes ships to get coffee here. We have other uses for most of our ships. And as for your French lamb chops—well, you'll get them. But maybe not every day and maybe not as many as you want till the war's over. But you won't have to live on turnips and horsemeat—you won't have to stand in line for hours for a piece of spoiled fish—

WOMAN: Why, I should say not! Why, that would kill me!

NARRATOR [*quietly*]: It has killed—quite a good many people in Europe. But it won't kill you. There'll be rationing and more rationing. There'll be shortages, here and there, at various times. The fighting men have to come first. But you'll be with us till the end of the war—a little thinner, maybe, and just as angry. You're lucky.

WOMAN: Lucky?

NARRATOR: I said—lucky. The Nazis' weapon is hunger. They've used it again and again. They proclaimed it only last October third at the Sportspalast in Berlin when Hermann Goering—fat Hermann who eats a dozen lobsters at a sitting got up and said—

GOERING: Aber wenn durch Feindeassnahmen Schwierigkeiten entstehen sollten, dann sollen alle wissen: Wenn es Hunger geben wird, dann nicht in Deutschland. Die Deutschen werden die letzten sein, die zu leiden haben.

[*Sound: Nazi crowd shouting "Sieg Heil"*]

NARRATOR: Hear him? He's saying—the rest of Europe may starve, but Germany shall eat. He's saying it to his slaves—the cheering slaves of the Nazi party. And now he's getting kittenish—listen . . .

GOERING [*chuckles*]: Nun, in den besetzten Gebieten kaufen die meisten Leute ihre Nahrungsmittle sowieso im Schleichhandel.

[*Sound: Hearty laughter of German crowd*]

NARRATOR: What was that? Oh—he was saying—after all, in the occupied countries, most of the people buy their food at the black market anyway. The black market—where an egg, if you can get it, costs more than a pair of shoes and where people risk their lives for a handful of dried beans. And his cheering slaves all laughed—that was the big joke. Wonder what the Italians thought about that—the Italians who liked their spaghetti and don't get it any more. Wonder what the Quislings thought—and the Lavals—and the grim-faced men who wait in hiding for the tocsin of revolt to sound. But—that was Hermann Goering—number two Nazi—October 4, 1942. Write it down. Remember it.

[*Music: Set American theme and paint under*]

NARRATOR: Just a day before, in Tylertown, Mississippi, there was another kind of meeting. Didn't get so very much attention except from the people who were there. But out of the piny woods and the red-clay acres, the farmers came—

Negroes and whites, men and women, 4-H Clubs, New Farmers, everybody. They brought their fried chicken and their doughnuts and they heard our Secretary of Agriculture, Claude Wickard, speak.

[*Music out*]

No—nobody made them come—they weren't driven there by gun butts. But they came to give thanks for the harvest of Walthall County, Mississippi—619 per cent more truck crops than last year—110 per cent more eggs and the rest of their record. And Wickard said:

WICKARD: American farm families are fighting for freedom, using food as a weapon. They can look back with satisfaction on what they have accomplished. Warehouses and granaries would not now be filled unless farmers had worked this season from sunup to sundown. The women and girls of farm families have done men's work in the fields and with livestock after their work in the home was done. And we are thankful to feed both the men of the United States who are fighting our battles and the men and women behind the lines who are backing up our fighting men . . .

What we did this year was only a beginning. Each month our Army and Navy need more food, our allies turn to us for more. And every month more men leave the farm to go to war or to jobs in city factories. Every month the supplies we need in farming grow harder to get. Next year farmers will have more to do and less to do it with. We have much need for future courage and endurance. All of the nation's farmers join with you in gratitude for the blessing of the past year, for the abundance of the harvest. They join with you in the resolve never to let up in the battle of production. The road ahead for farmers is long and difficult but it is the only road that leads to victory.

NARRATOR: No—you needn't even applaud. Nobody has

to applaud in this country. Nobody has to say "Sieg Heil!" But—there's the difference.

GOERING [*echo*]: Wenn es hunger geben wird, dann nicht in Deutschland!

NARRATOR: In Berlin—it's Goering saying the rest of Europe may starve—but Germany shall eat. In American— it's the farmer saying. . . .

FARM VOICE: Food for our men . . . for our allies . . . for the starving and the oppressed . . . food for freedom!

NARRATOR: Their weapon—hunger. Our weapon—food. And not just food in a glut-unplanned production—tearing up the buffalo grass to sow wheat and start another dust bowl—planting Victory gardens hit or miss without thought to the future. Our food production was planned as our military effort was planned. We did it this way.

ADMINIS. VOICE: Three months before Pearl Harbor, the Food for Freedom goals were announced. They called for the greatest farm output in history. After Pearl Harbor they were raised higher. And because we were ready, we are getting all-out production of the war crops we need. Today, we have selective service in crops. We produce according to the needs of our fighting men, allies, and civilians on the home front. We are cashing in on a decade of better care of our soil. And this year, farmers are harvesting far more than we have produced in any other year. That is the record.

NARRATOR: It had to be planned out ahead. Had to be because you can't hurry nature. You can cut down your shipbuilding time to less than five days, but it still takes months to farrow a pig and raise him to market and two years to raise a dairy cow. You can work inside a factory no matter how bad the weather is, but hail and drought and storm can ruin any crop. No, the government planned ahead and set goals for the farmers. It said:

ADMINIS. VOICE: We're going to need more than 4 billion dozen eggs. Can you produce them?

FARM VOICE: Ask us.

ADMINIS. VOICE: And 10½ million more hogs? How about that?

FARM VOICE: Ask me.

ADMINIS. VOICE: Peanuts—we need the oil and the cake —3 million acres more of peanuts than last year.

FARM VOICE: We'll plant 'em.

ADMINIS. VOICE: Soybeans—need 'em for oil. Need 'em for a dozen uses. Need 9 million acres—half again as many as last year.

FARM VOICE: Never had much to do with soybeans, but I hear they can be raised.

ADMINIS. VOICE [*a little incredulously*]: And suppose we said—enough milk to float all the navies of the United Nations? Enough cheese to pave the Lincoln Highway?

FARM VOICE: We're Americans, aren't we? Let's go.

[*Sound: Slap of reins on back of a mule*]

VOICE: Giddyap, mule, we're breaking ground.

[*Sound: Grind of tractor*]

VOICE: Just gimme a hand with that tractor, Bill. Got to make that quota. Got to hustle.

[*Sound: Squeal of pig. Barnyard*]

VOICE: Come on, you little pig. You got to eat and grow fat. The soldiers like ham and bacon.

[*Sound: Moo of cow*]

VOICE: Soo, boss. Give down. You can't go dry on Uncle Sam.

VOICE: Five brood sows and thirty-two pigs.

VOICE: Two hundred heavy-breed chicks.

VOICE: Sixty acres of barley.

FARM VOICE: Strike it up on your fiddle, Billy. Strike it up for Woodville, California.

[*Music: Key chords and into song*]

VOICE [*singing*]: Troopers need truck man, scratch that ground

Get your hands in a stalk and your back bowed down.

ᛁ   CHORUS: Ain't got a rifle, only got a hoe

But will we let the troops starve? No, chile, no!

VOICE: Get your back bowed down so the folks can say

He bowed his back for the U. S. A.

CHORUS: Scrouge your hands raw now—hide and all—

Won't need 'em no way till next fall.

VOICE: Ain't got a rifle, ain't got a gun,

But I'll break my back till this war gets won.

CHORUS: Hack at that Axis! Use your hoe!

Gonna let the troops starve? No, chile, no!

[*Music: Pick up orchestra and reprise in bg and paint*]

NARRATOR: And that was the way they went about it—from the migrant workers in Woodville Camp to all the other farmers through the length and breadth of the nation. And the total farm goal was met—and many of the crop goals were exceeded. We can't show you all of it. We can't show you the spring rains and the summer heat and the day that starts with sunup and never gets done till the evening chores are done. We can't show you the woman's side of it —the canning and the preserving and the ache in the back at the end of the day. We can't show you the quiet war of six million sunburnt Americans, fighting for the land and with the land—the war that never gets in the communiqués but the very backbone of our war. We can't make you hear corn grow—we can't make you hear the young wheat sucking in the rain. We can't even give you a sound effect for a soybean.

[*Music: out*]

SOUND EFFECTS MAN: We can too.

NARRATOR: What's that?

SOUND EFFECTS MAN: We can too give a sound effect for a soybean.

NARRATOR: All right—all right—let's hear it.

SOUND EFFECTS MAN: Hold on to your hats. Here she goes.

[*Sound: Rattle of antitank fire*]

NARRATOR: You mean to tell me that's what a soybean sounds like?

SOUND EFFECTS MAN: Sure. Two pounds of soybean oil make enough glycerin to fire five antitank shells. Want to hear what a bale of wool sounds like?

[*Sound: Boom of gun*]

NARRATOR: But that's an eighty-millimeter gun!

SOUND EFFECTS MAN: Right. And as much wool goes into an eighty-millimeter gun mount as goes into a woman's skirt. And here.

[*Sound: Bomb explosion*]

SOUND EFFECTS MAN: Castor-oil bean. Use the oil as a binder for bombs. Sorry I can't show you more but I'm working on a new sound effect. Got to get back to it.

NARRATOR: What's that?

SOUND EFFECTS MAN: Hitler's last squeal when he hears the Yanks have landed. Got to hurry on that one. So long.

NARRATOR [*dazed*]: So long.

[*Music: Punctuate and resolve and continue under*]

NARRATOR: Well, that was quite a little interruption. But he's right. A farm today is a munitions factory too. The boy who enlists on a farm enlists in an army. The farmer who does his work well is part of an army. No matter how far away he is from the front line, he's backing up that front line. No matter what is said about him by those who do not know him—no matter how much he is misrepresented by petty and selfish politicians and blocs—no matter how he is scarified by men who have never hardened their hands by a day's work in the field and would break their backs if they had to pitch hay for an hour. He is still a soldier of the earth. The man of whom Jefferson said, "Surely those who labor in the earth are the chosen people of God"—of whom Webster said: "When tillage begins, other arts follow. The farmers are the founders of human civilization." They will not fail and are not failing this nation.

[*Music out*]

They have met their huge quotas for this year with faith and good will. Next year they will be called upon for even more. And that means—

A VOICE: It means work and sweat. We know that. It means doing without and making other things do. Parity prices? All right—that's up to the government. But, parity prices or not—we're farmers. We'll do our share.

A VOICE: Farm labor's scarce now—and getting scarcer. Sure, our boys want to enlist. And lots of them have. But, we've got to keep some on the farm or you won't have your crops.

A VOICE: Farm machinery—well, we can patch and make do. We're willing. Sure, we'd like repairs . . . But repairs or not, we'll go on. Because, if Hitler wins that's the end of my farm and me.

A VOICE: Sure. We know skunks when we see them—and we know weasels. We know what to do with a dog when he slobbers in the dog days and we know just where to nail up the hides of vermin.

A VOICE: Those Russian farmers—had to burn their standing wheat. Must have been hard to do that. But I know how they felt.

A VOICE: I hear from my cousin in the old country. I hear how they steal his stock and laugh in his face. We're against you, Mr. Hitler—and we're staying against you.

VOICE: We're against you, Mr. Tojo—and all your smart little Zeros that had to swipe other folks' land and bomb them out of their homes. I heard about you from my nephew . . . I know what he says.

[*Music: Sneak in and faint under*]

FARM VOICE: We're against you all, you Axis—against you for life or death. We're free men here in this country and we mean to stay free. We've got good neighbors here and we mean to keep them. We're not waving banners and parading—you don't get much time to parade when you work a farm. But we're buying war bonds and collecting scrap, from the kids' old rubber dolly to the iron out in the barn. And outside that and on top of it, we're raising the food to sink you and swamp you and finish you—the corn and the hogs, the fruit and the cotton and the wheat and everything that grows. We're going to take a gang plow and plow your New Order under—we're going to take your planned hunger and drown it in Jersey milk. And when we've done it, maybe, the earth will be decent again. . . . But, we're in for the duration and don't you forget it—and we're six million Americans and the country started with us. We give thanks today, for the men who are fighting for us—a lot of them came from our farms. We give thanks for the land we work and the crops that grow from that land. We give thanks for the stock and the animals—they aren't human though sometimes you might think so—but they're part of the farm and the life, so I guess we won't leave them out. But, most of all we give thanks for the biggest crop we raise here—and that crop's name is freedom.

[*Music: Up and out*]

Well, that's my speech for Thanksgiving Day. You got something to say, mother?

[*Music: Sneak in and paint under*]

FARM WOMAN: I've got just this to say. When I married a farmer I married good times and bad times. I married hail-storms and drought and the worry about the loan and the work that has to be done no matter how tired you feel. It hasn't always been easy and it isn't too easy now. Times enough—I've wanted to sit down and rest, like a picture in a magazine. But I don't care. I'm part of this country—me and millions of women like me—and we don't get medals for it, though one time I did get a blue ribbon for my watermelon preserve. As the text says, we know what our hands have done. And we mean to keep on doing it. At first I didn't hardly see how I could be grateful this Thanksgiving—with the war and everything and our eldest boy in the Navy. He wanted to go and he did, but I keep remembering. But I thought it all over to myself, and I am grateful to Almighty God that this country lives and grows. I'm grateful to foreign friends—friends I'll never see in my life—who are fighting with us and for us. I wouldn't even be able to talk some of their languages but I'm grateful just the same. I'm grateful for us getting united and keeping united—that's the way we ought to be. I'm grateful we could raise what we've raised— And I know what went into it—and we'll keep on. For my house and what we've got, for my children and what they are, for the neighbors and friends that lend a hand in trouble, and for what I see every day—the land and its growing . . . I'm grateful.

[*Music: Up and out*]

Will you ask the blessing, father?

FARM VOICE: Good Lord, bless this food and us to thy service.

FARM WOMAN: Good Lord, bless and defend this country and us to its service.

MAN: Amen.

WOMAN: Amen.

ALL: Amen.

NARRATOR: And so say we all. Amen!

[*Music: Sweep up and into song with chorus*]

CHORUS [*singing*]: Come, ye thankful people, come,
Raise the song of harvest home;
All is safely gathered in,
Ere the winter storms begin;
God, our Maker doth provide
For our wants to be supplied;
Come to God's own temple, come,
Raise the song of harvest home.

[*Music and chorus to curtain and out*]

(CURTAIN)

THEY BURNED THE BOOKS

Broadcast under the auspices of the Council on Books in Wartime and the Writers' War Board, on Monday evening, May 11, 1942, over the NBC Network.

The production was under the direction of Lester O'Keefe; special music composed by Tom Bennett, and the orchestra under the direction of Josef Stopak.

THEY BURNED THE BOOKS

[Program opens with a rush of Fire-Music, swelling and then subsiding; as music subsides, a heavy, ominous bell tolls ONE]

        VOICES *[Tense and whispering]*

            One!

          BELL *[Tolls]*

          VOICES

            Two!

          BELL *[Tolls]*

          VOICES

           Three!

        [Fire-Music Up and Down]

       BELL *[Louder and quicker]*

         VOICES *[Quicker]*

          Seven!

BELL [*Tolls*]
VOICES
Eight!
BELL [*Tolls*]
VOICES
Nine!
[*Fire-Music*]
NARRATOR: Nine! Nine iron years of terror and evil!
Nine years since a fire was lighted in a public square, in
Berlin.
Nine years since the burning of the books! Do you re-
member?
Write it down in your calendars, May 10, 1933,
And write it down in red by the light of fire.
    [*Crackle of flames, not too big*]
These are people who work by fire.
The Reichstag went up in flames that February
And in March they got their majority and moved in,
The storm-troopers, the heroes of the beer-hall Putsch,
The boys with a taste for beatings and executions,
The limping doctor, the swollen ex-Army pilot,
Gangster and bravo, hoodlum and trigger-man,
Led by the screaming voice that is war and hate,
Moved in on Germany like a cloud of locusts,
Having planned and plotted for long.
They strangled the German Republic and moved in.
    [*Crackle of flames*]
—And people said, "Well, that's interesting, isn't it?"
"Intéressant, n'est-ce pas?"
"My dear fellow, this fellow Hitler, quite extrord'nary.
Wonder what the beggar's up to?"
                                    Or people said,
"I see by the papers they had an election in Germany.

Seem to have lots of elections over there.
Say, what do you know about this bank-holiday, Joe?
If you need some cash, I've got a couple of bucks,
But the banks are bound to reopen."

That was March fifth. They burned the books May tenth.

Why bother about the books?
Why bother to go back to that fateful year,
Year that prepared the blood-purge and the wars,
The death of Austria, the trick of Munich,
The bombers over the defenseless towns,
And all we know and all that must be fought
Here, now and always till the score is paid
And from its grim recital pick one instance
Of calculated wrong?
A book's a book. It's paper, ink and print.
If you stab it, it won't bleed.
If you beat it, it won't bruise.
If you burn it, it won't scream.
      [*Crackle of flames*]
Burn a few books—burn hundreds—burn a million—
What difference does that make?
      VOICE OF SCHILLER [*firm, masculine and thoughtful*]:
It does to me.
Excuse me, sir—my name is Friedrich Schiller,
A name once not unknown in Germany,
One of the glories, so they said, of Germany,
A Germany these robbers never knew.
Over a century and a half ago
I spoke and wrote of freedom.
I spoke against oppressors and dictators.
I spoke for every man who lifts his head

And will not bow to tyrants.
And, though I died, my poems and plays spoke on
In every tongue, in every land for freedom,
For that's what books can do.
And now, today, in the land where I was born—

NAZI VOICE: The play, *William Tell,* by Friedrich
Schiller shall no longer be performed on the stage. It glori-
fies a dangerous and unseemly spirit of revolt against con-
querors. It shall no longer be performed on the German
stage. This is an order!

NARRATOR: That's what they do. That's what they do to
the mind.
That's what they do to the books of their own great dead.
That's how they foul the present and the past,
Shut the dead mouth so that it cannot speak
Because it spoke far too well.
Now, here's another ghost,
Pale, frail, satirical, a mocking spirit,
But with the light of freedom in his eyes.
Your name, brave ghost?

HEINE'S VOICE [*sharp and humorous*]: My name? It's
Heinrich Heine.
Born to much sorrow, born to be a man.
Out of my laughter and my heart's despair,
I made my little songs—such simple songs
A child could understand them—and grown men
Remember them and love them all their lives.
Some were so funny! Some were pitiful.
And some were trumpet calls for liberty,
For, though I couldn't fight, I was a fighter,
And when my time had come to die, I said
After long torment in my mattress-grave,
"Bury me with a sword upon my coffin

For I have been a soldier of humanity!"

NARRATOR: A soldier of humanity
And you deserved that name,
But now—today—what happens to your songs?

HEINE: Well—there was one about a lorelei,
Just a small song. It went—let's see—like this—
[*He hums the first bars of "The Lorelei" to faint background music*]
You've heard it, maybe? Many people sing it.
They sang it many years along the Rhine.
They sing it still.

NARRATOR: Still?

HEINE: Oh, yes. That one of mine they—haven't
burned.
That would be just a little difficult.
Too many Germans know the words by heart.
So, with totalitarian courtesy,
They've kept the song—and blotted out my name.
You see—I was a Jew.

NAZI VOICE: New editions of the works of the Jew,
Heinrich Heine, are not desirable. In all textbooks and
anthologies where the words of the song "The Lorelei" appear, the name of the Jew, Heine, shall be omitted and the
author given as "Author Unknown."

HEINE [*mocking*]: Author well-known—since 1828.
Author unknown—since 1933.

NARRATOR: That's what they do to soldiers of humanity!
That's how they rob the soldier of his sword,
The dead man of the one thing he may keep,
His name—his very name!
Don't think that's all.
Don't think it's just the singers and the poets!

Light the flames—light the flames—and hear them roar!
See what the flames consume!

[*Fire-Music in. Tramp of feet. Crackle of flames*]

They're coming now—the men with the tramping feet,
The hard-faced boys with the truncheons—the new order!
The flames they've lighted howl and leap in the square.
You can't set fire to a Reichstag every day,
But the pyre that they light today shall fling its shadows
In flame and shadow over the whole round world.
Hear them tramp! They're coming! They bring the books
        to the fire!

NAZI VOICE: The books of the Jew, Albert Einstein—to
the flames!

OTHER VOICES: Sieg Heil!

[*Noise of flames*]

NARRATOR: Einstein, the scientist,
Who thought in universes.
Einstein, the man we honor in our land.

NAZI VOICE: To the flames with him—to the flames!

VOICES: Sieg Heil!

NAZI VOICE: The books of Sigmund Freud—to the
flames!

[*Noise of flames*]

NARRATOR: Freud, prober of the riddles of man's mind,
World-known, world famous.

[*Noise of flames*]

NAZI VOICE: To the flames—the flames!

Burn them—we don't want thought—we don't want mind.
We want one will, one leader and one folk!

HEINE'S VOICE [*cutting in*]: One vast, inexorable
stupidity!

NAZI VOICE: Who said that? Gag him—burn him—to
the flames!

To the flames with Heinrich Mann and Thomas Mann,
Gorki the Russian, Schnitzler the Austrian,
Hemingway, Dreiser, the Americans,
And now, to the flames with this!

VOICES: Sieg Heil!

[*Noise of flames*]

NARRATOR: That is the Bible. Would you burn God's word?

NAZI VOICE: We need no Bible but the words of the Leader.
We have no god except the German gods.
We have the tanks, the guns, the bombs, the planes
And that shall be enough!

VOICES: Sieg Heil! Sieg Heil!

HEINE'S VOICE: And yet there shall be weeping for this burning,
Weeping throughout your land.
The weeping of poor women and old men
Who loved and trusted in the word of God
And now are worse than homeless in your world
For you have taken their last failing hope,
The promise of their Father and their Lord.

NAZI VOICE: How dare you speak?
Exile and Jew, how dare you speak to us?

HEINE: I speak for all humanity in chains,
Exile, Jew, Christian—for the prison-camps,
And those who dwell in them and bide their time—
For the dishonored, for the dispossessed,
For those you have ground like wheat.
I speak for every honest man of God,
Driven from his own pulpit, by your might,
And for those who saw that happen—and remember it.

I speak for the dark earth and the mute voices
And yet I speak humanity unbound.
    NAZI VOICE: You? You are just a singer,
A worthless singer!
    HEINE: True.
And that is why I speak, because I know,
Being a singer, what moves every heart.
I speak with little barbs and little songs
So simple any child can understand
Just what they say—and yet so memorable
Once you have heard them you will not forget them
But they will stay within your memory,
Sweet as first love, salt as the tears of man,
Free as the winds of heaven in the sky.
And you do well to try to shut my mouth
For, while one little song of mine remains,
All that you hate and would destroy remains,
Humor and grace and human tenderness,
Laughter and mockery and the bare sword,
The sword I wanted on my lonely coffin,
The sword of liberty.
    NAZI VOICE: We'll shut your mouth!
We'll find you in the graveyard where you lie,
Dig up your rotten bones and scatter them
Till there is nobody in all the world
Who's heard of Heinrich Heine!
    HEINE [*mocking*]: Dig deep! Dig well!
Scatter my dust, break up my burial stone,
Erase my name with all your thoroughness,
Your lumbering, fat-headed, thoroughness,
Smelling of beer and bombs!
And yet, while there's a book, there will be Heine!

There will be Heine, laughing at you still,
Laughing with all the free—with all the free!
  [*His voice fades. Music*]
  NARRATOR: Yes.
There will be Heine. There will be all those
Whose words lift up man's heart.
But only if we choose.
This battle is not just a battle of lands,
A war of conquest, a balance-of-power war.
It is a battle for the mind of man
Not only for his body. It will decide
What you and you and you can think and say,
Plan, dream, and hope for in your inmost minds
For the next thousand years.
Decide whether man goes forward towards the light,
Stumbling and striving, clumsy—but a man—
Or back to the dark ages, the dark gods,
The old barbaric forest that is fear.
Books are not men, and yet they are alive.
They are man's memory and his aspiration,
The link between his present and his past,
The tools he builds with, all the hoarded thoughts,
Winnowed and sifted from a million minds,
Living and dead to guide him on his way.
Suppose it happened here.
Suppose the books were burned here.
This is a school, somewhere in America.
This is the kind of school we've always had,
Argued about, paid taxes for, kept on with,
Because we want our kids to know some things.
Suppose it happened here.
  [*Typical school bell buzzing. Shuffle of feet, buzz of voices*] [*Bell stops*]

VOICE OF A WOMAN TEACHER, MISS WINSLOW: The class will come to order.

[*Noise of class settling down*]

MISS WINSLOW: This morning we are going to discuss some of the basic American ideas on which our nation was founded—freedom, tolerance, liberty under law. To start the discussion, I am going to ask Joe Barnes to recite the Gettysburg Address to us. Do you think you can do that without looking at your book too much, Joe?

JOE BARNES [*an adolescent voice*]: I—I guess so, Miss Winslow. Studied it last night.

MISS WINSLOW: Very well, Joe. You may begin.

JOE BARNES: The Gettysburg Address. By Abraham Lincoln. "Fourscore and seven years ago our fathers brought forth on this continent a new nation, conceived in liberty and dedicated to the proposition that all men are created equal."

NAZI VOICE: Stop!

JOE BARNES [*continuing uncertainly*]: Now we are engaged—we are engaged—

NAZI VOICE: Stop! The words of the Gettysburg Address can no longer be studied in any school of our glorious new order!

[*Rustle and protesting murmur from class*]

MISS WINSLOW: But those are the words of Lincoln!

JOE BARNES: But Miss Winslow told me—

NAZI VOICE: Miss Winslow is no longer your teacher. I am your teacher. Attention!

[*Rustle of class*]

When I give the command, you will rise and bring your textbooks to my desk. All this nonsense of freedom and tolerance—that is finished. All this nonsense of men being equal—that is finished. We shall give you new textbooks.

The old ones will be burned in the schoolyard. Are there any questions?

[*Silence*]

NAZI VOICE: Good. The new order does not like questions.

MISS WINSLOW: I protest! This is infamous! You can't know what you're doing! I have taught here for twenty years!

NAZI VOICE: So I understand. That is a long time, Miss Winslow—too long. You deserve a long rest. We'll see you get it. No, you needn't bother to say goodbye to your students. Guards! Take the woman away!

[*Music up and down*]

NARRATOR: Impossible? Fantastic? Sounds that way.
Ask the teachers and books of occupied France,
France, that loved letters—France, once the light of
    Europe—
Read the list of books the French—can't read any more.
What sort of books?
Well, there are all kinds, of course, from detective stories
To the life of a great French queen. But here, for instance,
Is a history of Poland—

NAZI VOICE: Suppressed.

NARRATOR: Why? Well, according to the New Order,
Poland has no history.

NAZI VOICE: Poland has no history.

NARRATOR: And here,
French History for Secondary Schools,
History of France, History of France and Europe,
Contemporary Europe, Legends and Fables
of France for Children—

NAZI VOICE: Suppressed. Withdrawn. On the blacklist.

NARRATOR: But these are not guns or daggers
Stored up against revolt. They're the commonplace
Textbooks, thumbed by a thousand schoolboy fingers,
Inkspotted, dogeared, drowsed above in classrooms,
Familiar and dull and mild.
They must be harmless enough.
   NAZI VOICE: They are not harmless. We know what we
are doing.
   NARRATOR: Yes. They know what they are doing.
They know, if you take the children of a country
And teach them nothing but lies about the world,
Give them no chance for argument or questions,
Give them no books that show another side,
No word of all the words that speak for freedom,
The man who grows from the child will believe the lies
And never hear of the truth.
                                        It's a simple plan,
As simple and efficient as arsenic.
Just rewrite all of the books to suit yourself
And the rest will follow in time—the beatings and burnings,
The massed, mechanical might and the metal men.
Would you like a sample of American history
Nazi style? Can you stand it? You'd better know
What it would be like for your children and their children.
You heard Joe Barnes give the Gettysburg Address.
This is what he'd be like if he'd never heard it
Or anything like it, ever—if all his books
Were the textbooks of the New Order
If our schoolbooks wore swastikas.

Come in Joe, will you?
Looks different in his brown shirt, doesn't he?
Can you tell us about American history, Joe?

Some—names—and dates—and people—

JOE BARNES [*in a mechanical, sullen voice*]: American history dates from the foundation of the New Order.

NARRATOR: Nothing before that?

JOE BARNES: Nothing important.

NARRATOR: Well, come, Joe, there must have been one or two things before that.

JOE BARNES: Nothing important.

NARRATOR: After all, for instance, the discovery of America. That was fairly important. Do you know anything about that?

JOE BARNES: Yes. That is in my book. [*Reciting mechanically*] America was discovered in 1492 by Christopher Columbus, an honorary Aryan.

NARRATOR: An honorary Aryan? I always thought he was an Italian.

JOE BARNES: That was before the New Order. He is now an honorary Aryan of the second class—like Mussolini and Hirohito.

NARRATOR: I wonder how he likes that. However—after Columbus—

JOE BARNES: There came the New Order.

NARRATOR: But weren't there just a few things in between? Wasn't there something called the Declaration of Independence?

JOE BARNES [*scornfully*]: Oh—that! Yes, there was that. But it was all wrong. It said everyone was entitled to life, liberty and the pursuit of happiness. That was all wrong.

NARRATOR: Who wrote it?

JOE BARNES: It is unimportant who wrote it. It is not in my book.

NARRATOR: Didn't you ever hear of a man named Thomas Jefferson?

JOE BARNES: Thomas Jefferson? No. There is no such man in my book.

NARRATOR: Or George Washington?

JOE BARNES: Yes, he was a general. But not a very good one. He was defeated by German might at the battle of Trenton. Afterwards he foolishly became President of the United States instead of ruling his country with a strong, mailed fist.

NARRATOR: But maybe he didn't believe in ruling people with a strong, mailed fist.

JOE BARNES [*impatiently*]: He may have had some such old-fashioned, sentimental ideas. That is why he is unimportant. The man to study in his period is Benedict Arnold —a man much ahead of his time.

NARRATOR: I always thought Benedict Arnold was a traitor to his country.

JOE BARNES: Traitor? What nonsense! He sensibly tried to collaborate with a stronger power in order to save his countrymen from the horrors of democracy and revolution. He is a very honorary Aryan of the first class, with star. We have many honorary Aryans just like Benedict Arnold.

NARRATOR: I wouldn't be a bit surprised. And—just one last question, Joe.

JOE BARNES: Yes. But hurry, please. I must attend a Strength Through Joy meeting—and it is necessary for me to clean my pistol, first.

NARRATOR: Did you ever hear of a man who said "Government of the people, by the people, for the people?"

JOE BARNES [*violently and fearfully*]: Certainly not! Of course not! It's a lie! You've been spying on me! My father did have the book but I never saw it! It's a long while ago and the teacher has been sent away! I know nothing about Abraham Linc——

[*Music up and down*]

NARRATOR: That's it. That's how they work.
That's what they do to kids.
That's the way they'd like to work here.

NAZI VOICE: That's it, my friend. You see, we can destroy
Houses with bombs and people with starvation,
Outflank defensive lines and tramp ahead.
We can destroy the spirit of a nation
With poisoned doubts and fears,
Erase its history, blot out its past,
Sully its famous names and substitute
Our words for all the words of liberty.
But, while there is a single man alive,
Hidden or starving, who somehow remembers
The vows of freedom, the undying words
That spoke for man's free mind,
Though they were said a thousand years ago,
Our conquest is not perfect.
                    They are terrible,
These immaterial and airy words,
Sharp as edged swords, infectious as the plague.
They travel silently from mind to mind,
Leaving no trace. They live in quiet books
You hardly would suspect unless our leader
Had wisely warned us of them. They hide and creep
In jokes and catchwords under our own noses,
In dots and dashes, in a bar of music.
    [*V motif in music*]
And, worse than all,
Within the silent eyes of hungry men,
Waiting their time, waiting their hungry time.
That's why they must be killed.

That's why we burn the books. That's why we burn
All knowledge, all the recollected thought
Gathered in patience through three thousand years
Of civilization. That knowledge is man's brain
And till we've taken an electric wire
And burned the brain cells from his very brain
So he will be a dumb and gaping slave,
We cannot win. And still we mean to win!
Get the fire ready! Bring the books to the fire!

    [*Fire-Music, fading into the tolling of a great bell*]

    NARRATOR: Nine years ago.

    [BELL *tolls*]

    NARRATOR: Nine years ago in Berlin.

    [BELL *tolls*]

    NARRATOR: Nine years ago in a public square in Berlin.

    [BELL *tolls*]

    NARRATOR: They burned the books and that was the be-
ginning.
We didn't know it then. We know it now.
Hear the books burn.

    [*Sound of flames*]

    VOICES: Einstein—to the fire!
Mann—Toller—Helen Keller—to the fire!
Old Testament and New—to the fire—to the fire!

    [*Fire-Music. Flames. Bell*]

    NARRATOR: This is in memory. This is in remembrance.
This is for all the lies that have been told.
The innocent blood, the blood that cries from the ground,
Rise up and speak, you voices!
Voices of dead and living, past and present,
Voices of gagged men, whispering through sore lips,
Voices of children, robbed of their small songs,
Strong voices, chanting of the rights of man,

Rebel and fighter, men of the free heart,
We, too, shall build a fire, though not in fear,
Revenge or barren hate, but such a great
And cleansing fire it shall leap through the world
Like leaping flame!
                    Freedom to speak and pray,
Freedom from want, and fear, freedom for all;
Freedom of thought, freedom of man's bold mind!
Who marches with us?
    SCHILLER: I am Friedrich Schiller
And I march with you in the cause of man.
    HEINE: I am the soldier of humanity,
The mocking smile upon the face of Time
That men called Heine. And I march with you.
    AN ENGLISH VOICE: My name is Milton. I am old and
blind.
I knew oppression and defeat and scorn
And the high justice of eternal God,
Paradise lost and paradise regained,
And I march with you.
    AN IRISH VOICE: My name is Jonathan Swift,
Dean of St. Patrick's, scourge of knaves and fools,
Though bitter indignation
Tore at my heart and cracked it till it broke,
I never had a patient mind for tyrants,
And I march with you.
    AN AMERICAN VOICE: I hailed my sunburnt children in
their youth,
Pioneers, pioneers!
I told them Walt would back them to the end.
I said they should be free. I sang democracy,
The new word, the new meaning, the bright day,
And I march with you!

FRENCH VOICE: The miserable shall be lifted up.
The tyrants all cast down.

SECOND ENGLISH VOICE: The Parliament of Man, the
Federation of the world.

SECOND AMERICAN VOICE: Well, maybe that'll take a
while to grow
(My name's Sam Clemens.)
But Pudd'nhead Wilson says
"Cauliflower is just a cabbage with a college education."
And so we might start in.
About this business, now.
I may have made a living, cracking jokes,
But one thing I did hate was cruelty.
One thing I did dislike was pompous fools
Treading on decent people. Count me in.

NARRATOR: Milton and Whitman, Tennyson and Swift,
Mark Twain and Hugo—every one who wrote
With a free pen in words of living fire,
From Plato, dreaming of his bright Republic,
To every exile walking in our streets,
Exiled for truth and faith.
And all of ours, all of our own today,
All those who speak for freedom.
These are our voices. These shall light our fire.
Light the bright candle that shall not be quenched,
That never has been quenched in all man's years
Although all darkness and all tyranny
Have tried to quench it.
                    Call the roll of those
Who tried to quench it!

A COLD, ECHOING VOICE: Darius, the Persian. Darius,
the Great King.

NARRATOR: Where is Darius?

COLD VOICE: Dead. Forgotten and dead.

COLD VOICE: Attila the Hun. Attila, devourer of peoples.

NARRATOR: Where is Attila?

COLD VOICE: Bones. Forgotten bones.

COLD VOICE: Alaric the Goth. Alaric, destroyer of Rome.

NARRATOR: Where is Alaric?

COLD VOICE: Dust. Forgotten dust.

NARRATOR: Adolf Hitler, born April 20, 1889.

WHISPERING VOICES: Adolf Hitler.

NARRATOR: Adolf Hitler, burner of books.

WHISPERING VOICES: Adolf Hitler.

NARRATOR: Adolf Hitler, destroyer of thought.

WHISPERING VOICES: Adolf Hitler.

[BELL *tolls*]

VOICES: Adolf Hitler, born 1889.

VOICES: Died. Died. Died. Died. Died.

NARRATOR: We are waiting, Adolf Hitler.

The books are waiting, Adolf Hitler.

The fire is waiting, Adolf Hitler.

The Lord God of Hosts is waiting, Adolf Hitler.

[*Music up to climax*]

(CURTAIN)

THE UNDEFENDED BORDER

Broadcast on the Cavalcade of America, NBC Red Network, December 18, 1940.

Raymond Massey played The Border Voice.

The program was directed by Homer Fickett, and the original musical score was composed by Don Voorhees.

THE UNDEFENDED BORDER

THE BORDER VOICE: All over the world, there are borders between countries. They may be rivers or mountains —they may be nothing more than lines on a map. But, in time of war, they are ravaged land—No Man's Land. And, in time of peace, the guns still look at each other. Between the wars, the grass grows back again, but sometimes it doesn't grow for long. And there are always soldiers.

But from New Brunswick to Puget Sound there runs a border between two great nations of proud people, individual people, people with their own customs and beliefs and ways, and that border has not one fort, not one ship of battle, not one hidden or usable gun. There is a lone cannon. And they point it out to tourists as a memory of the past. The cannon is rusted now and covered with moss.

The little boys on both sides of the border climb over it and are not afraid. And there are the voices of people talking across the border—voices like Bill Carter. He was born in Chicago.

BILL CARTER: Yeah, I lived in the States until 1916. Then I enlisted over the border. Told the recruiting sergeant I was from Montreal, but I guess he knew where I came from. They used to call me the Yank. I was wounded and gassed but my girl married me just the same. Now we're living in Vancouver and I've got a nice little business there.

THE BORDER VOICE: People—people. All through the years, millions of people both sides of the border. Take Sally Forbes. Sally came from North Dakota. They married young out there in the 70's, and Sally was like the others. She was only sixteen when she married Randall Forbes.

SALLY FORBES: Randall! Always said I snatched him bald-headed—but you know how a man talks. Well, we homesteaded near Calgary and the years went by so fast. Randall Jr.'s a doctor in Baltimore and Harry teaches at McGill. Yes, the children are scattered now. If you're asking about the border, well, I know it's there. But you can't build a fence between a woman and her children.

THE BORDER VOICE: Just the voices of people talking across the border. The voices of people who have known how to share a continent together in Peace and Good Will through the Sun and the Rain and the Years. Voices of men and women with the same sort of beliefs, the same sort of courage even seventy years ago, voices like our own.

MACEACHERN [*Scotch Irish*]: My name's Hugh MacEachern—there were four MacEacherns of my name before me in Canada. Yet I fought four years in the Army of the Potomac—and there were fifty thousand like me, first and

last, in the Union Armies. They gave me bounty money—
but that was not why I went—I felt it was a fight for freedom. When it was done, I came home. I worked my lands.
I gave my life and strength to Canada. But all my life I
remembered the men I had fought beside. When they came
to my house, they were welcome; when I went to their
house, I was welcome. May it ever be so between the two
houses.

THE BORDER VOICE: And yet it wasn't always so. There
had been a war in 1812. A war between two peoples who
spoke the same tongue, and, like all wars, it left scars. Let's
stand on the Canadian side of a great water. It is summer in
the year 1817. There's a small boy launching a toy boat. His
name is Jock McKinstry.

BOY: Do you like my new boat, father?

JOCK: Aye, you've done a good job on her, son. She's
a fine little sloop of war.

BOY: Billy Ross and I are going to have a big battle
and sink all the Yankees.

JOCK: Son—look across the water there.

BOY [*puzzled*]: Yes, father.

JOCK: Do you mind the boy Jimmy Hunter you played
with in the old days? He lives over there. And now maybe
he's building a boat, too—a fine little sloop of war—on his
side of the lake.

BOY: Father—I don't understand—

JOCK: Jimmy's father was *my* friend too, son. And here,
on both sides of the border, we've a free great land to dwell
in. So what would you do, now war's over?

BOY: I'd send him a peace belt—the way the Indians do.

JOCK: Now that's a suggestion. But would he take it,
do you think?

BOY: Oh, of course he would—you *have* to take a peace belt.

JOCK [*taps side of boat*]: But here's your fine big sloop of war, son. [*Music sneak*] And it's not boys that build them —it s grown men—both sides of the border.

[*Music up and down. Noise of hammering*]

THE BORDER VOICE: Yes—it isn't boys—but grown men —both sides of the border. Hear the hammers! Shipwrights' hammers, carpenters' hammers, calking hammers, hammers on fresh-smelling wood and bright iron. Hammers by the ports and shores of Ontario and Erie and Champlain. The pleasant harbors, the pine-smelling beaches, Hammers, building the ships of war! Lakes? These are not lakes but oceans. They must be defended.

CHANT [*Canadian*]: Lead pills for the Yankees. They'll soon have enough With grape and with round shot, We'll give them hot stuff.

1ST VOICE [*Canadian*]: British Admiralty. Lake Ontario. Ship of the line, St. Lawrence, 110 guns.

2ND VOICE [*Canadian*]: The Psyche, 50 guns. The Princess Charlotte, 40.

3RD VOICE [*Canadian*]: Sailmakers—

4TH VOICE [*Canadian*]: Powder monkeys—

1ST VOICE [*Canadian*]: Carpenters—

2ND VOICE [*Canadian*]: 74-gun frigates. 74-gun frigates. Prepare. Prepare. Prepare.

[*Music up and down*]

THE BORDER VOICE: And as it was on one shore, so it was on the other.

CHANT [*U.S.*]: And have you heard of Perry? Of Oliver Hazard Perry?

Oh, have you heard of Perry?
And his famous victory?

1ST VOICE [*U.S.*]: United States Navy Department. Lake Ontario. The Superior, 44 guns. The Mohawk, 32 guns. The General Pike, 24 guns.

2ND VOICE [*U.S.*]: Get ready. Prepare.

3RD VOICE [*U.S.*]: Militia—

4TH VOICE [*U.S.*]: The Niagara. The Jefferson. 18 guns.

1ST VOICE [*U.S.*]: Forts—

2ND VOICE [*U.S.*]: Men. Arms. Frigates. Cannon.

[*Music up and down*]

CANADIAN-AMERICAN CHORUS [*rising*]: Cannon. Cannon. Cannon. Cannon. Cannon. Cannon. Cannon. Cannon.

[*Musical climax*]

THE BORDER VOICE: And that's the way it starts. [*Music*] That's the way we know it starts. The border must be kept with forts, ships and cannon. Come and see how Americans felt about it on their side of the lake in 1817.

[*Swish of water, the Yankee side beaching a canoe*]

JEAN-BAPTISTE [*shouting off*]: Jim Hunter! Howdy, Jim Hunter!

HUNTER: Jean-Baptiste! Come on shore, you old pirate —ain't seen you in a coon's age.

JEAN-BAPTISTE [*coming in*]: Well, well, I'm glad to see you, Jim Hunter.

HUNTER: Well, I'm glad to see you. New canoe?

JEAN-BAPTISTE: Finest dam' canoe on the lakes.

HUNTER: Don't doubt that none. Well, Jean-Baptiste, what's the news?

JEAN-BAPTISTE: Oh, she's about the same. New baby— good year for beaver.

HUNTER: Uh-hunh. You fight in the war?

JEAN-BAPTISTE: Sure, I fight. I fight like six men at Chateaugay.

HUNTER: Fought at Lundy's Lane, myself.

JEAN-BAPTISTE [*he laughs*]: Say, you know what I do at Chateaugay? I capture my own cousin!

HUNTER: Huh?

JEAN-BAPTISTE: Sure—he's lying on the ground with bullet in his leg. He's Baptiste-Jean, Henri-Louis-David-Ligonier. Like me. Same name. Afterwards he go home to Maine—he write me a letter— [*Snap of fingers*] Oh, there I am, one big fool! I've got letter for you, Jim Hunter—I forget—

HUNTER: A letter. Hm. Feels sizable. Who gave it to you?

JEAN-BAPTISTE: Jock McKinstry. You open up now. I take answer back.

[*Noise of opening package*]

HUNTER: Why—it's a wampum belt. A white belt. That's old, that is. That's Huron work.

JEAN-BAPTISTE: The white belt—she mean peace—

HUNTER: Peace—and already they're building ships of war again on the lakes. I wish the people in London and Washington could know how we people on the border feel. Someone ought to tell 'em.

JEAN-BAPTISTE: You are right there, my friend.

HUNTER: Well, there's only one way to do that. Tell 'em. Fellows like us can't go across the ocean to London. But a man could get to Washington if he'd aim to. [*Music sneak*] I wonder where Washington is. They say it's a long way away . . .

[*Music up and down*]

THE BORDER VOICE: It was a long way to Washington. But there was the pole star to go by and the old Indian trails. That was the forest when Jim Hunter left the banks of the great lake. Beyond, south and east, lay rolling green valleys not yet claimed from the wilderness. And Jim Hunter slept under the stars, head pillowed on his pack, in the wilderness. Through the Onondaga section he strode; and the hunting good on the finger lakes; and the twigs crackling underfoot when Jim Hunter sighted a clump of cabins through the trees.

[*Footsteps along the road. Dog barking*]

HUNTER [*calling out*]: Halloo, the house!

SETTLER [*over dog*]: Halloo yourself!

HUNTER: What's the name of this place, stranger?

SETTLER: It ain't got a name. It's mine.

HUNTER: What's the nearest town?

SETTLER: Tioga.

HUNTER: How far?

SETTLER: Quite a piece.

HUNTER: Got any meal?

SETTLER: I might have.

HUNTER: I'll swap you three prime squirrel for some. I've come quite a ways and I'm tired of eating squirrel.

SETTLER: It's a trade. Come in a' light.

[*Music*]

THE BORDER VOICE: A long way to Washington. The moccasins wearing thin. But there were friends in the wilderness. Countrymen. And all the rich sweet valley of the Susquehanna lay ahead. Through Sunbury, not stopping the night. The next night rain, dripping through the boughs. Jim Hunter went on. Gray morning into late dusky evening. Days had become weeks. Then—Harrisburg, a settlement still sleeping in the curve of the blue river, the mountains, misty beyond. And at York, a signpost pointing

to Baltimore, a city. It was the first city Jim Hunter had
ever seen. Just forty miles from Washington. Washington!

And now, in the muddy and straggling Washington of
1817, two other men meet to talk of a distant border. They
aren't remarkable men. You don't read much about Richard
Rush in the history books. Richard Rush—Acting Secretary
of State—not Secretary, you know, just Acting. And Sir
Charles Bagot—British Envoy Extraordinary to the United
States—for a while—with no great name in history. English
—American—two honest men of good will.

[*Clink of glasses*]

RUSH: A toast, Sir Charles—to His Highness, the Prince
Regent!

BAGOT: To the President of the United States!

[*They drink*]

RUSH: And now, Sir Charles. Shall we proceed to our
business?

BAGOT: With pleasure.

RUSH: Correct me, sir, if I am in error—but the question between our countries seems to resolve itself to this—
what armed forces, if any, our respective governments intend to keep on the border between the United States and
Canada.

BAGOT: Between Canada and the United States.

RUSH: I accept the correction. Now, Mr. Adams feels
that these armaments should be greatly reduced.

BAGOT: Lord Castlereagh, unofficially, has long been
of the same opinion.

RUSH [*fade in echo*]: At the same time, Sir Charles, we
have laid down the keels of certain ships.

BAGOT: His Majesty's Navy has not been wholly idle.

[*We hear again the faint sound of hammers, swelling*]

WHISPERED VOICE [*on dynamic mike*]: British Admiralty. The St. Lawrence. 110 guns.

2ND WHISPERED VOICE [*on dynamic mike*]: Prepare. Sailmakers. Powder monkeys.

RUSH: Sir Charles, I do not control the military policy of my government—but as a citizen I can say we are profoundly disturbed by the recent developments in American waters.

WHISPERED VOICE [*on dynamic mike*]: The Niagara. Badly damaged. Refit. Prepare.

BAGOT: *Our* citizens along the Maine border are greatly disturbed by what seems to them *American aggression!*

2ND WHISPERED VOICE [*on dynamic mike*]: Get ready. The Psyche, 50 guns. Frigates.

RUSH: Maine is defending her just claims, Sir Charles!

WHISPERED VOICE [*on dynamic mike*]: The Superior, 44 guns. The Mohawk, 32 guns—

BAGOT: Her just claims to Canada's fisheries, Mr. Rush?

2ND WHISPERED VOICE [*on dynamic mike*]: Prepare. Cannon. Cannon.

RUSH: The fisheries question has nothing to do with it, Sir Charles! The recent—and most unwarranted attack on an American vessel—

1ST WHISPERED VOICE [*on dynamic mike*]: Cannon—

2ND WHISPERED VOICE [*on dynamic mike*]: Cannon—

3RD WHISPERED VOICE [*on dynamic mike*]: Cannon—

1ST AND 2ND WHISPERED VOICES [*on dynamic mike*]: Cannon—

1ST, 2ND, AND 3RD WHISPERED VOICES [*on dynamic mike*]: Cannon. Cannon. Cannon. [*Other voices join in and build*] Cannon. Cannon. Cannon. Cannon. Cannon.

[*Voices rise to a cutoff*]

BAGOT: I—I confess I was growing heated. Your pardon, sir. Another glass of your excellent Madeira.

RUSH: With pleasure.

[*A pause*]

RUSH [*in a different voice*]: Come, Sir Charles. Let us drop diplomatic formalities for the moment. That border line between us is not just a set of marks upon a map. Let me show you something I received from that border today. [*Scrape of desk drawer opening*] Here. Do you know it's significance?

BAGOT: A belt of Indian wampum.

RUSH: It was brought me this morning by an American trapper. May I ask you to hear his story?

BAGOT: Why, of course—

RUSH [*rings bell, to servant who answers*]: Show Mr. Hunter in.

NEGRO: Yes, Mistah Rush.

[*Door, etc.*]

RUSH: Sir Charles, this is James Hunter, one of our frontiersmen. Mr. Hunter—Sir Charles Bagot, His Majesty's Envoy Extraordinary.

BAGOT: Your obedient servant, Mr. Hunter. Mr. Rush has just shown me this very interesting belt.

HUNTER: Yes, sir. Indian work. Means peace.

BAGOT: And how, if I may ask you, is the feeling between the citizens on the border?

HUNTER: Depends. We ain't tame on the border. Neither side. But we'd like to be shut of fighting. That's why I brought the belt.

BAGOT: You'd like to be shut of fighting. May I ask you why?

HUNTER: Why, mister, it's like this. You see, here's me, one side of the lake—and here's Jock McKinstry, the other side. He's got his ideas and I've got mine. He's loyal to King and Crown and I'm loyal to the United States—but, we get along fine. Well, Jock McKinstry sent me the belt. He's Scotch and he don't talk much but he meant what he said. He meant peace. Well, I know he couldn't get to London—that's across water—so I figured I'd better come here.

BAGOT: If I may ask, Mr. Hunter, how long did the journey take you?

HUNTER: One pair of moccasins—call it a moon and a half—

BAGOT: One pair of—

RUSH: Perhaps forty days, Sir Charles. On foot.

BAGOT: Forty days!

RUSH: Tell me, Mr. Hunter—and you may speak quite freely—what force do you think would be sufficient to maintain peace and order on the lakes?

HUNTER: That's for you folks to say.

BAGOT: But we want to know what you think—you and Jock McKinstry.

HUNTER: Well, if it was me and Jock McKinstry—I'd say just one boat each side.

RUSH: And what of forts—and soldiers—

HUNTER: Well, forts and soldiers—you see, they're for enemies. We've fought, but we ain't enemies. We'll differ and we'll always differ. But we want to be friends.

BAGOT: I believe you, Mr. Hunter. May I keep the white belt? I should like to send it to London—and thank you.

[*Music*]

THE BORDER VOICE: And finally the Rush-Bagot agreement was signed, in April, 1817. James Monroe was president then. James Monroe of the Monroe Doctrine. And because of the sense and good will of two peoples the hammers stopped on the Great Lakes. And a bored clerk read in the Senate of the United States . . .

VOICE OF CLERK: "Naval forces to be maintained upon the American Lakes by His Majesty's Government and the Government of the United States shall be confined, on Lake Ontario, to one vessel not exceeding one hundred tons burden and armed with one eighteen pound cannon . . ."

THE BORDER VOICE: The lone cannon. And back and forth, back and forth, across the border, the tide of human beings has ebbed and flowed. Trapper, trader, farmer, merchant, woman and man. It's they who have kept the peace and the freedom. The border's men and women.

[*Music up and down*]

THE BORDER VOICE: I am the voice of the border. I was born under the Maple Leaf. I was born under the Stars and Stripes. I'm people who are used to space and wide skies—to an old and dear tradition and the wind that blows over a new world. The Douglas fir and the redwood, the trillium and the number one hard wheat—all these are in the veins of my people. The gray stones of Quebec are part of them and the old French speech—the rolling Dakota plains and the warm, wheat-growing summers—the springs of the Mississippi and the shining bay of Vancouver and the rocky shield of the Laurentians, the necklace around the North Pole. Where there is space and freedom, love of law and love of justice, you will find my people. We live next each other and we're used to each other's ways. We swing the same kind of ax and we drive in the same kind of cars. We marry back and forth and the children don't quarrel. We've had a lot of history together and our wide earth remembers it. We've had William Lyon Mackenzie and John Brown. We've had Sir Wilfrid Laurier and Teddy

Roosevelt and John A. MacDonald and Abe Lincoln. We've
had folks who tried to sow dissension too, but they never
raised a crop and they never will. For when we say "freedom" we mean it, and we have faith in the people. Do-
minion—Republic—we have faith in the people. And together we'll keep that faith, for the years and the children
still to be.

[*Music and chorus of voices*]

AMERICAN VOICES: We built a house for freedom here
And free it shall remain.

CANADIAN VOICES: We built it out of Northern pine
And Manitoba grain.

MIXED VOICES: We built it with our hearts and lives
From Puget Sound to Maine.

CHORUS: The House was built in freedom's name
And so it shall abide
For your tall sons and my tall sons,
Whatever may betide,
We'll keep the peace our fathers kept
And keep it side by side.

THE BORDER VOICE: We built it with the broad ax
And the shining rails of steel,
The birchbark of the voyageurs,
The creaking wagon wheel,
We built it with the best we had
For the loyal and the leal.

CHORUS: While rock endures and pine endures
And Western corn grows tall,
With your strong sons and my strong sons
We shall maintain it all.
The house we built in freedom's name,
The house that shall not fall.

[*Orchestra and chorus fade under*]

THE BORDER VOICE: The great house of freedom,
The house that shall not fall.
[*Orchestra and chorus up and finish*]

(CURTAIN)

LISTEN TO THE PEOPLE

Broadcast in co-operation with the Council For Democracy over the NBC Blue Network, July 4, 1941.

The original cast included Henry Hull, Howard Lindsay, Otto Preminger, Katharine Emery and Robert Gray.

The program was directed by Lester O'Keefe, and the musical score was composed and conducted by Vaclav Moravan.

LISTEN TO THE PEOPLE

[Orchestra: Music up and out]
NARRATOR: This is Independence Day,
Fourth of July, the day we mean to keep,
Whatever happens and whatever falls
Out of a sky grown strange;
This is firecracker day for sunburnt kids,
The day of the parade,
Slambanging down the street.
Listen to the parade!
There's J. K. Burney's float,
Red-white-and-blue crepe-paper on the wheels,
The Fire Department and the local Grange,
There are the pretty girls with their hair curled
Who represent the Thirteen Colonies,
The Spirit of East Greenwich, Betsy Ross,

137

Democracy, or just some pretty girls.
There are the veterans and the Legion Post
(Their feet are going to hurt when they get home),
The band, the flag, the band, the usual crowd,
Good-humored, watching, hot,
Silent a second as the flag goes by,
Kidding the local cop and eating popsicles,
Jack Brown and Rosie Shapiro and Dan Shay,
Paul Bunchick and the Greek who runs the Greek's,
The black-eyed children out of Sicily,
The girls who giggle and the boys who push,
All of them there and all of them a nation.
And, afterwards,
There'll be ice cream and fireworks and a speech
By Somebody the Honorable Who,
The lovers will pair off in the kind dark
And Tessie Jones, our honor graduate,
Will read the declaration.
That's how it is. It's always been that way.
That's our Fourth of July, through war and peace,
That's our Fourth of July.

And a lean farmer on a stony farm
Came home from mowing, buttoned up his shirt
And walked ten miles to town,
Musket in hand.
He didn't know the sky was falling down
And, it may be, he didn't know so much.
But people oughtn't to be pushed around
By kings or any such.
A workman in the city dropped his tools.
An ordinary, small-town kind of man
Found himself standing in the April sun,

One of a ragged line
Against the skilled professionals of war,
The matchless infantry who could not fail,
Not for the profit, not to conquer worlds,
Not for the pomp or the heroic tale
But first, and principally, since he was sore.
They could do things in quite a lot of places,
They shouldn't do them here, in Lexington.

He looked around and saw his neighbors' faces . . .

    AN ANGRY VOICE: *Disperse, ye villains! Why don't you disperse?*

    A CALM VOICE: *Stand your ground, men. Don't fire unless fired upon. But if they mean to have a war, let it begin here!*

    NARRATOR [*resuming*]: Well, that was that. And later, when he died
Of fever or a bullet in the guts,
Bad generalship, starvation, dirty wounds
Or any one of all the thousand things
That kill a man in wars,
He didn't die handsome but he did die free
And maybe that meant something. It could be.
Oh, it's not pretty! Say it all you like!
It isn't a bit pretty. Not one bit.
But that is how the liberty was won.
That paid for the firecrackers and the band.

    A YOUNG VOICE [*radical*]: Well, what do you mean, you dope?
Don't you know this is an imperialist, capitalist country, don't you?
Don't you know it's all done with mirrors and the bosses get the gravy, don't you?

Suppose some old guy with chin whiskers did get his pants
shot off at a place called Lexington?
What does it mean to me?

AN OLDER VOICE [*conservative*]: My dear fellow, I my-
self am a son of a son of a son of the American Revolution,
But I can only view the present situation with the gravest
alarm.
Because we are rapidly drifting into a dictatorship
And it isn't my kind of dictatorship, what's more.
The Constitution is dead and labor doesn't know its place,
And then there's all that gold buried at Fort Knox
And the taxes—oh, oh, oh!
Why, what's the use of a defense-contract if you can't make
money out of your country?
Things are bad—things are very bad.
Already my Aunt Emmeline has had to shoot her third
footman.
(He broke his leg passing cocktails and it was really a kind-
ness.)
And, if you let the working classes buy coal, they'll only
fill bathtubs with it.
Don't you realize the gravity of the situation, don't you?
Won't you hide your head in a bucket and telegraph your
congressman, opposing everything possible, including peace
and war?

A TOTALITARIAN VOICE [*persuasive*]: My worthy Ameri-
can listeners.
I am giving you one more chance.
Don't you know that we are completely invincible, don't
you?
Won't you just admit that we are the wave of the future,
won't you?
You are a very nice, mongrel, disgusting people—

But, naturally, you need new leadership.

We can supply it. We've sent the same brand to fourteen nations.

It comes in the shape of a bomb and it beats as it sweeps as it cleans.

For those of you who like order, we can supply order.

We give the order. You take it.

For those of you who like efficiency, we can supply efficiency.

Look what we did to Coventry and Rotterdam!

For those of you who like Benito Mussolini, we can supply. He's down three doors at the desk marked Second Vice-President.

Now be sensible—give up this corrupt and stupid nonsense of democracy.

And you can have the crumbs from our table and a trusty's job in our world-jail.

RADICAL VOICE: Forget everything but the class struggle. Forget democracy.

CONSERVATIVE VOICE: Hate and distrust your own government. Whisper, hate and never look forward.

Look back wistfully to the good old, grand old days—the days when the

Boys said "The public be damned!" and got away with it.

Democracy's a nasty word, invented by the Reds.

TOTALITARIAN VOICE: Just a little collaboration and you too can be part of the New Order.

You too can have fine new concentration camps and shoes made out of wood pulp. You too can be as peaceful as Poland, as happy and gay as France. Just a little collaboration. We have so many things to give you.

We can give you your own Hess, your own Himmler, your own Goering—all home-grown and wrapped in cellophane. We've done it elsewhere. If you'll help, we can do it here.

    RADICAL VOICE: Democracy's a fake—

    CONSERVATIVE: Democracy's a mistake—

    TOTALITARIAN: Democracy is finished. We are the future.

    [*Music up and ominous*]

    NARRATOR [*resuming*]: The sky is dark, now, over the parade.

The sky's an altered sky, a sky that might be.

There's J. K. Burney's float
With funny-colored paper on the wheels
Or no—excuse me—used to be J.K.'s
But the store's under different management
Like quite a lot of stores.
You see, J.K. got up in church one day,
After it all had happened and walked out,
The day they instituted the new order.
They had a meeting. Held it in the church.
He just walked out. That's all.
That's all there is to say about J.K.
Though I remember just the way he looked,
White-faced and chin stuck out.
I think they could have let the church alone.
It's kind of dreary, shutting up the church.
But don't you say I said so. Don't you say!
Listen to the parade!
There are the pretty girls with their hair curled,
Back from the labor camp.
They represent the League of Strength Through Joy.
At least, I guess it's that.
No, they don't go to high school any more.

They get told where they go. We all get told.
And, now and then, it happens like Jack Brown,
Nice fellow, Jack. Ran the gas station here.
But he was married to a You-Know-Who.
Fond of her, too.
I don't know why we never used to mind.
Why, she walked round like anybody else,
Kept her kids clean and joined the Ladies' Social.
Just shows you, doesn't it? But that's all done.
And you won't see her in the crowd today,
Her or the kids or Jack,
Unless you look six feet under the ground,
The lime-washed ground, the bitter prison ground
That hides the martyrs and the innocent,
And you won't see Dan Shay.
Dan was a Union man
And now we don't have Unions any more.
They wouldn't even let him take his specs,
The day the troopers came around for him.
    [*Half hysterically*]
Listen to the parade!
The marching, marching, marching feet,
All with the same hard stamp!
The bands, the bands, the bands, the flags, the flags,
The sharp, mechanical, inhuman cheer
Dragged from the straining throats of the stiff crowd!
It's Independence—sorry, my mistake!—
It's National Day—the Day of the New Order!
We let it happen—we forgot the old
Bleak words of common sense, "Unite or Die,"
And the clock struck—and the bad dream was here.

    A VOICE: But you can't do this to me! I subscribed to
the Party funds!

A VOICE: You can't do this to me. We got laws. We got courts. We got unions.

A VOICE: You can't do this to me. Why, I believe in Karl Marx!

A VOICE: You can't do this to me. The Constitution forbids it.

A VOICE: I was always glad to co-operate.

A VOICE: It looked to me like good business.

A VOICE: It looked to me like the class struggle.

A VOICE: It looked to me like peace in our time.

TOTALITARIAN VOICE: Thank you, ladies and gentlemen. Democracy is finished. You are finished. We are the present!

[*Music up and down*]

NARRATOR: That is one voice. You've heard it. Don't forget it.
And don't forget it can be slick or harsh,
Violent or crooning, but it's still the same,
And it means death.

Are there no other voices? None at all?
No voice at all out of the long parade
That marched so many years,
Out of the passion of the Puritans,
The creaking of the wagons going west,
The guns of Sharpsburg, the unnumbered dead,
Out of the baffled and bewildered hosts
Who came here for a freedom hardly known.
Out of the bowels of the immigrant ship,
The strange, sick voyage, the cheating and the scorn
And yet, at the end, Liberty.
Liberty with a torch in her right hand,
Slowly worked out, deceived a thousand times,
But never quite forgotten, always growing,

Growing like wheat and corn.
"I remember a man named Abe Lincoln.
I remember the words he used to say."
Oh, we can call on Lincoln and Tom Paine,
Adams and Jefferson.
Call on the great words spoken that remain
Like the great stars of evening, the fixed stars,
But that is not enough.
The dead are mighty and are part of us
And yet the dead are dead.
　　This is our world,
Our time, our choice, our anguish, our decision.
This is our world. We have to make it now,
A hundred and thirty millions of us have to
And make it well, or suffer the bad dream.
What have we got to say?
　　A WOMAN'S VOICE: I don't know, I'm a woman with a
house,
I do my work. I take care of my man.
I've got a right to say how things should be.
I've got a right to have my kids grow up
The way they ought to grow. Don't stop me there.
Don't tread on me, don't hinder me, don't cross me.
I made my kids myself. I haven't got
Big words to tell about them.
But, if you ask about democracy,
Democracy's the growing and the bearing,
Mouth at the breast and child still to be born.
Democracy is kids and the green grass.
　　NARRATOR: What have we got to say,
People, you people?
　　MAN'S VOICE: I guess I haven't thought about it much.
I been too busy. Way I figure it

It's this way. We've got something. If it's crummy
The bunch of us can change what we don't like
In our own way and mean it.
I got a cousin back in the old country.
He says it's swell there but he couldn't change
A button on his pants without an order
From somebody's pet horse. Maybe he likes it.
I'm sticking here. That's all. Well, sign me off.

NARRATOR: People, you people, living everywhere,
Sioux Falls and Saugatuck and Texarkana,
Memphis and Goshen, Harrodsburg and Troy,
People who live at postmarks with queer names,
Blue Eye and Rawhide, Santa Claus and Troublesome,
People by rivers, people of the plains,
People whose contour plows bring back the grass
To a dust-bitten and dishonored earth,
And those who farm the hillside acres still
And raise up fortitude between the stones,
Millions in cities, millions in the towns,
People who spit a mile from their front doors
And gangling kids, ballplaying in the street,
All races and all stocks, all creeds and cries,
And yet one people, one, and always striving. . . .

A MAN: I'm on relief
I know what they say about us on relief,
Those who never were there.
All the same, we made the park.
We made the road and the check-dam and the culvert.
Our names are not on the tablets. Forget our names.
But, when you drive on the road, reemmber us, also.
Remember Johnny Lombardo and his pick,
Remember us, when you build democracy,
For we, too, were part and are part.

NARRATOR: One nation, one.
And the voices of young and old, of all who have faith,
Jostling and mingling, speaking from the ground,
Speaking from the old houses and the pride,
Speaking from the deep hollows of the heart.
MAN'S VOICE: I was born in '63.
There were many then who despaired of the Republic,
Many fine and solid citizens.
They had good and plausible reasons and were eloquent.
I grew up in the Age of Brass, the Age of Steel.
I have known and heard of three wars.
All through my life, whenever the skies were dark,
There came to me many fine and solid citizens,
Wringing their hands, despairing of the Republic,
Because we couldn't do this and shouldn't do that.
And yet, each time, I saw the Republic grow
Like a great elm tree, through each fault and failure,
And spread its branches over all the people.
Look at the morning sun. There is the Republic.
Not yesterday, but there, the breaking day.
TOTALITARIAN VOICE: But, my worthy American listeners.
All this is degenerate talk.
The future rolls like a wave and you cannot fight it.
A VOICE: Who says we can't?
A VOICE: Who says so?
A VOICE: How does he get that way?
A VOICE: You mean to tell me
A little shrimp like that could run the world,
A guy with a trick mustache and a bum salute,
Run us, run you and me?
TOTALITARIAN VOICE: You mistake me.
Others have often made the same mistake

Often and often and in many countries.
I never play upon a people's strength.
I play upon their weaknesses and fears.
I make their doubts my allies and my spies.
I have a most convincing mask of peace
Painted by experts, for one kind of sucker,
And for another—I'm a businessman,
Straight from the shoulder, talking trade and markets
And much misunderstood.
I touch this man upon his pocketbook,
That man upon his hatred for his boss,
That man upon his fear.
I offer everything, for offering's cheap.
I make no claims until I make the claims.
I'm always satisfied until I'm not
Which happens rather rapidly to those
Who think I could be satisfied with less
Than a dismembered and digested world.
My secret weapon is no secret weapon.
It is to turn all men against all men
For my own purposes. It is to use
Good men to do my work without their knowledge,
Not only the secret traitor and the spy.
It is to raise a question and a doubt
Where there was faith. It is to subjugate
Men's minds before their bodies feel the steel.
It is to use
All envy, all despair, all prejudice
For my own work.
If you've an envy or a prejudice
I'll play on it and use it to your ruin.
My generals are General Distrust,
General Fear, General Half-A-Heart,

General It's-Too-Late,
General Greed and Major General Hate,
And they go walking in civilian clothes
In your own streets and whisper in your ears.
I won't be beaten just by sitting tight.
They tried that out in France. I won't be beaten
By hiding in the dark and making faces,
And certainly I never will be beaten
By those who rather like my kind of world,
Or, if not like it, think that it must come,
Those who have wings and burrow in the ground.
For I'm not betting only on the tanks,
The guns, the planes, the bombers,
But on your own division and disunion.
On your own minds and hearts to let me in,
For, if that happens, all I wish for happens.
So what have you to say?
What have you got to bet against my bet?
Where's your one voice?

    AMERICAN VOICE: Our voice is not one voice but many
voices.
Not one man's, not the greatest, but the people's.
The blue sky and the forty-eight States of the people.
Many in easy times but one in the pinch
And that's what some folks forget.
Our voice is all the objectors and dissenters
And they sink and are lost in the groundswell of the people
Once the people rouse, once the people wake and listen.
People, you people, growing everywhere,
What have you got to say?
There's a smart boy here with a question and he wants an-
    swers.
What have you got to say?

A VOICE: We are the people, listen to us now.

A VOICE: Says you we're puny? We built Boulder Dam,
We built Grand Coulee and the TVA.
We built them out of freedom and our sweat.

VOICE: Says you we're faint of heart and little of mind?
We poured like wheat through the gaps of the Appala-
chians.
We made the seas of wheat, the seas of corn.
We made five States a sea of wheat and corn.

VOICE [_laughing_]: We built the cities and the sky-
scrapers.
All the proud steel. We built them up so high
The eagles lost their way.

VOICE: That's us. When did you do a job like that?

VOICE: Wasn't enough.

VOICE: No, and you bet it wasn't.
Not with the apple-sellers in the streets,
Not with the empty shops, the hungry men.
But we learned some things in that darkness and kept free.
We didn't fold up and yell for a dictator.
We built, even in the darkness. We learned our trade
By the licks we took and we're building different now.

VOICE: We lost our way for a while but we've found our
way.
We know it and we'll hold it and we'll keep it.
We'll tell it to the world. We're saying it.

VOICE: Freedom to speak and pray.

VOICE: Freedom from want and fear.

VOICE: That's what we're building.

                         Now and here and now.

NARRATOR: People, you people, risen and awake. . . .

VOICE: That's what we're building and we'll build it
here.

That's what we're building and we'll build it now,
Build it and make it shine across the world,
A refuge and a fortress and a hope,
Breaking old chains and laughing in the sun.
This is the people's cause, the people's might.
We have set up a standard for the free
And it shall not go down.
That's why we drill the plate and turn the wheel,
Build the big planes.
That's why a million and a half of us
Learn here and now how free men stand in arms.
Don't tread on us, don't hinder us, don't cross us.
We won't have tyranny here.

VOICE: We don't give one long low hoot for your master race.
We think your slick new order's a bowl of raspberries.
We'll pick the small and the free and the enduring,
Wherever we find them and wherever they are.
We won't have tyranny here.

VOICE: We'll stick by Rosie Shapiro and Dan Shay
Paul Bunchick and the Greek who runs the Greek's,
And all of 'em like that, wherever they are.
We'll stick by the worn old stones in Salem churchyard,
The Jamestown church and the bones of the Alamo.
We won't have tyranny here.

VOICE: It's a long way out of the past and long way forward.
It's a tough way too, and there's plenty of trouble in it.
It's a black storm crowding the sky and a cold wind blow-
ing,
Blowing upon us all.
See it and face it. That's the way it is.
That's the way it'll be for a time and a time.

Even the easy may have little ease.

Even the meek may suffer in their meekness.

But we've ridden out storms before and we'll ride out this one,

Ride it out and get through.

It won't be done by the greedy and the go-easies.

It'll be done by the river of the people,

The mountain of the people, the great plain

Grown to the wheat of the people,

It'll be done by the proud walker, Democracy,

The walker in proud shoes.

Get on your feet, Americans, and say it!

Forget your grievances, wherever you are,

The little yesterday's hates and the last year's discord,

This is your land, this is your independence,

This is the people's cause, the people's might.

Say it and speak it loud, United, free . . .

MANY VOICES: United, free.

VOICE: Whatever happens and whatever falls,

We pledge ourselves to liberty and faith.

MANY VOICES: To liberty and faith.

VOICE: We pledge ourselves to justice, law and hope

And a free government by our own men

For us, our children and our children's children.

MANY VOICES: For us, our children and our children's children.

VOICE: Not for an old dead world but a new world rising.

VOICE: For the toil, the struggle, the hope and the great goal.

[*Music up and down*]

NARRATOR: You've heard the long parade

And all the voices that cry out against it.
 [*Quietly*]
What do the people say?
Well, you've just heard some questions and some answers,
Not all, of course. No man can say that's all.
But look in your own minds and memories
And find out what you find and what you'd keep.
It's time we did that and it won't be earlier.
I don't know what each one of you will find,
It may be only half a dozen words
Carved on a stone, carved deeper in the heart,
It might be all a life, but look and find it—
Sun on Key West, snow on New Hampshire hills,
Warm rain on Georgia and the Texas wind
Blowing across an empire and all part,
All one, all indivisible and one—
Find it and keep it and hold on to it,
For there's a buried thing in all of us,
Deeper than all the noise of the parade,
The thing the haters never understand
And never will, the habit of the free.
Out of the flesh, out of the minds and hearts
Of thousand upon thousand common men,
Cranks, martyrs, starry-eyed enthusiasts,
Slow-spoken neighbors, hard to push around,
Women whose hands were gentle with their kids
And men with a cold passion for mere justice.
We made this thing, this dream,
This land unsatisfied by little ways,
This peaceless vision, groping for the stars,
Not as a huge devouring machine
Rolling and clanking with remorseless force
Over submitted bodies and the dead

But as live earth where anything could grow,
Your crankiness, my notions and his dream,
Grow and be looked at, grow and live or die.
But get their chance of growing and the sun.
We made it and we make it and it's ours.
We shall maintain it. It shall be sustained.

ALL VOICES UP: WE SHALL MAINTAIN IT. IT SHALL BE SUSTAINED.

[*Music up to climax*]

(CURTAIN)

A CHILD IS BORN

Originally broadcast on the Cavalcade of America program over the NBC Network the night of December 21, 1942. The program was produced and directed by Homer Fickett, and music was conducted by Don Voorhees.

In the original cast Alfred Lunt played the part of the Innkeeper and Lynn Fontanne played the Innkeeper's Wife.

The script was repeated by popular request on the same program the evening of December 20, 1943, with Helen Hayes and Philip Merivale in the leading roles.

A CHILD IS BORN

[*Music, as broadcast opens. It fades. Narrator speaks.*]

NARRATOR: I'm your narrator. It's my task to say
Just where and how things happen in our play,
Set the bare stage with words instead of props
And keep on talking till the curtain drops.
So you shall know, as well as our poor skill
Can show you, whether it is warm or chill,
Indoors or out, a battle or a fair,
In this, our viewless theater of the air.
It's an old task—old as the human heart,
Old as those bygone players and their art
Who, in old days when faith was nearer earth,
Played out the mystery of Jesus' birth

In hall or village green or market square
For all who chose to come and see them there,
And, if they knew that King Herod, in his crown,
Was really Wat, the cobbler of the town,
And Tom, the fool, played Abraham the Wise,
They did not care. They saw with other eyes.
The story was their own—not far away,
As real as if it happened yesterday,
Full of all awe and wonder yet so near,
A marvelous thing that could have happened here
In their own town—a star that could have blazed
On their own shepherds, leaving them amazed,
Frightened and questioning and following still
To the bare stable—and the miracle.

So we, tonight, who are your players too,
Ask but to tell that selfsame tale to you
In our own words, the plain and simple speech
Of human beings, talking each to each,
Troubled with their own cares, not always wise,
And yet, at moments, looking toward the skies.

The time is—time. The place is anywhere.
The voices speak to you across the air
To say that once again a child is born.
A child is born.
"I pray you all, give us your audience
And hear this matter with reverence."
     [*Music*]
There is a town where men and women live
Their lives as people do in troubled times,
Times when the world is shaken. There is an inn.
A woman sings there in the early morning.

[*Music, fading into the voice of a woman—the inn-*
keeper's wife—singing as she goes about her house-
hold tasks]

INNKEEPER'S WIFE: In Bethlehem of Judea
There shall be born a child,
A child born of woman
And yet undefiled.

He shall not come to riches,
To riches and might,
But in the bare stable
He shall be Man's light.

He shall not come to conquest,
The conquest of kings,
But in the bare stable
He shall judge all things.

King Herod, King Herod,
Now what will you say
Of the child in the stable
This cold winter day?

I hear the wind blowing
Across the bare thorn,
I fear not King Herod
If this child may be born.

[*Sound of steps coming down a flight of stone stairs. A*
man's voice, rough and suspicious—the voice of the
innkeeper. The innkeeper is middle-aged—his wife
somewhat younger]

INNKEEPER: Singing again! I told you not to sing!
WIFE: I'm sorry. I forgot.

INNKEEPER: Forgot? That's fine!
That's wonderful! That answers everything!
The times are hard enough and bad enough
For anyone who tries to keep an inn,
Get enough bread to stick in his own mouth
And keep things going, somehow, in his town.
The country's occupied. We have no country.
You've heard of that, perhaps?
You've seen their soldiers, haven't you? You know
Just what can happen to our sort of people
Once there's a little trouble? Answer me!
    WIFE [*wearily*]: I've seen. I know.
    INNKEEPER: You've seen. You know. And you keep singing songs!
Not ordinary songs—the kind of songs
That might bring in a little bit of trade,
Songs with a kind of pleasant wink in them
That make full men forget the price of the wine,
The kind of songs a handsome girl can sing
After their dinner to good customers
—And, thanks to me, the inn still has a few!—
Oh, no! You have to sing rebellious songs
About King Herod!
    WIFE: I'm sorry. I forgot.
    INNKEEPER: Sorry? Forgot? You're always saying that!
Is it your business what King Herod does?
Is it your place to sing against King Herod?
    WIFE: I think that he must be a wicked man.
A very wicked man.
    INNKEEPER: Oh, la, la, la!
Sometimes *I* think your ways will drive me mad.
Are you a statesman or a general?
Do you pretend to know the ins and outs

Of politics and why the great folk do
The things they do—and why we have to bear them?
Because it's we—we—we
Who have to bear them, first and last and always,
In every country and in every time.
They grind us like dry wheat between the stones.
Don't you know that?

WIFE: I know that, somehow, kings
Should not be wicked and grind down the people.
I know that kings like Herod should not be.

INNKEEPER: All right—all right. I'm not denying that.
I'm reasonable enough. I know the world.
I'm willing to admit to anyone
At least behind closed doors
    [*He drops his voice*]
That Herod isn't quite my sort of king
And that I don't approve of all he does.
Still, there he is. He's king. How will it help
If I go out and write on someone's wall
    [*In a whisper*]
"Down with King Herod!"
    [*His voice comes up again*]
What's it worth?
The cross for me, the whipping post for you,
The inn burned down, the village fined for treason,
Just because one man didn't like King Herod.
For that's the way things are.

WIFE: Yet there are men—

INNKEEPER: Oh yes, I know—fanatics, rabble, fools,
Outcasts of war, misfits, rebellious souls,
Seekers of some vague kingdom in the stars—
They hide out in the hills and stir up trouble,
Call themselves prophets, too, and prophesy

That something new is coming to the world,
The Lord knows what!
   Well, it's a long time coming,
And, meanwhile, we're the wheat between the stones.
 WIFE: Something must come.
 INNKEEPER: Believe it if you choose,
But, meantime, if we're clever, we can live
And even thrive a little—clever wheat
That slips between the grinding stones and grows
In little green blade-sprinkles on the ground.
At least, if you'll not sing subversive songs
To other people but your poor old husband.
 [*Changing tone*]
Come, wife, I've got some news.
I didn't mean to be so angry with you.
You've some queer fancies in that head of yours
—Lord, don't I know!—but you're still the tall girl
With the grave eyes and the brook-running voice
I took without a dower or a price
Out of your father's house because—oh, well—
Because you came. And they've not been so bad,
The years since then. Now have they?
 WIFE: No.
 INNKEEPER: That's right.
Give us a kiss.
 [*Pause*]
   I couldn't help the child.
I know you think of that, this time of year.
He was my son, too, and I think of him.
I couldn't help his dying.
 WIFE: No, my husband.
 INNKEEPER: He stretched his little arms to me and died.
And yet I had the priest—the high priest, too.

I didn't spare the money.

 WIFE: No, my husband.

I am a barren bough. I think and sing

And am a barren bough.

 INNKEEPER: Oh, come, come, come!

 WIFE: The fault is mine. I had my joyous season,

My season of full ripening and fruit

And then the silence and the aching breast.

I thought I would have children. I was wrong,

But my flesh aches to think I do not have them.

I did not mean to speak of this at all.

I do not speak of it. I will be good.

There is much left—so much.

The kindness and the bond that lasts the years

And all the small and treasurable things

That make up life and living. Do not care

So much. I have forgotten. I'll sing softly,

Not sing at all. It was long past and gone.

Tell me your news. Is it good news?

 INNKEEPER [*eagerly*]: The best!

The prefect comes to dinner here tonight

With all his officers—oh yes, I know,

The enemy—of course, the enemy—

But someone has to feed them.

 WIFE: And they'll pay?

 INNKEEPER: Cash.

 WIFE: On the nail?

 INNKEEPER: Yes.

 WIFE: Good.

 INNKEEPER: I thought you'd say so.

Oh, we'll make no great profit—not tonight—

I've seen the bill of fare they asked of me,

Quails, in midwinter! Well, we'll give them—quails!

And charge them for them, too! You know the trick?
WIFE: Yes.
INNKEEPER: They must be well served. I'll care for that,
The honest innkeeper, the thoughtful man,
Asking, "Your worship, pray another glass
Of our poor wine! Your worship, is the roast
Done to your worship's taste? Oh, nay, nay, nay,
Your worship, all was settled in the bill,
So do not spoil my servants with largesse,
Your worship!"—And he won't. He pinches pennies.
But, once he's come here, he will come again,
And we shall live, not die, and put some coin,
Some solid, enemy and lovely coin
Under the hearthstone, eh?
Spoil the Egyptians, eh?
[*He laughs*]
That's my war and my battle and my faith.
The war of every sane and solid man
And, even if we have no child to follow us,
It shall be won, I tell you!
[*There is a knock at the outer door*]
Hark! What's that?
I'll go—the maids aren't up yet—lazybones!
[*The knock is repeated, imperatively*]
INNKEEPER [*grumbling*]: A minute—just a minute!
It's early yet—you needn't beat the door down.
This is an honest inn.
[*He shoots the bolts and opens the door, while speaking*]
Good morning.
SOLDIER'S VOICE: Hail Caesar! Are you the keeper of this
inn?
INNKEEPER: Yes, sir.
SOLDIER: Orders from the prefect. No other guests shall

be entertained at your inn tonight after sundown. The prefect wishes all the rooms to be at the disposal of his guests.

INNKEEPER: All the rooms?

SOLDIER: You understand plain Latin, don't you?

INNKEEPER: Yes, sir, but—

SOLDIER: Well?

INNKEEPER: Sir, when the prefect first commanded me,
There was a party of my countrymen
Engaged for a small room—he'd hear no noise—
No noise at all—

SOLDIER: This is the prefect's feast—the Saturnalia—
You've heard your orders.

INNKEEPER: Yes, sir. Yes, indeed, sir.

SOLDIER: See they are carried out! No other guests! Hail
Caesar!

INNKEEPER [*feebly*]: Hail Caesar!

[*He slams the door*]
Well, that's pleasant.
All rooms at the disposal of the prefect!
No other guests! I'll have to warn Ben-Ezra.
But he's a sound man—he will understand.
We'll cook his mutton here and send it to him.
And the wine, too—a bottle of good wine—
The second best and let the prefect pay for it!
That will make up. No other guests. Remember
No other guests!

WIFE: I will remember.

INNKEEPER: Do so.
It is an order. Now, about the quail.
You'll make the sauce. That's the important thing.
A crow can taste like quail, with a good sauce.
You have your herbs?

WIFE: Yes.

INNKEEPER: Well then, begin, begin!
It's morning and we haven't too much time
And the day's bitter cold. Well, all the better.
They'll drink the more but—all this work to do
And the fire barely started! Sarah! Leah!
Where are those lazy servants? Where's the fish?
Where's the new bread? Why haven't we begun?
Leah and Sarah, come and help your mistress!
I'll rouse the fools! There's work to do today!
     [*He stamps up the stairs. She moves about her business*]
     WIFE [*singing*]: In Bethlehem of Judea
There was an inn also.
There was no room within it
For any but the foe.

No child might be born there.
No bud come to bloom.
For there was no chamber
And there was no room.
     [*Her voice fades off into music which swells up and
       down*]
     NARRATOR: And the day passed and night fell on the
town,
Silent and still and cold. The houses lay
Huddled and dark beneath the watching stars
And only the inn windows streamed with light—
     [*Fade into offstage noise of a big party going on up-
       stairs*]
     1ST VOICE [*offstage*]: Ha, ha, ha! And then the Cilician
said to the Ethiopian. He said—
     2ND VOICE [*offstage*]: Well, I remember when we first
took over Macedonia. There was a girl there—

3D VOICE [*offstage*]: Quiet, gentlemen, quiet—the prefect wishes to say a few words—

PREFECT'S VOICE [*off*]: Gentlemen—men of Rome—mindful of Rome's historic destiny—and of our good friend King Herod—who has chosen alliance with Rome rather than a useless struggle—keep them under with a firm hand—

SARAH: What is he saying up there?

LEAH: I don't know.
I don't know the big words. The soldier said—

SARAH: You and your soldier!

LEAH: Oh, he's not so bad.
He brought me a trinket—see!

SARAH: You and your Roman trinkets! I hate serving them.
I'd like to spit in their cups each time I serve them.

LEAH: You wouldn't dare!

SARAH: Wouldn't I, though?
[*There are steps on the stairs as the innkeeper comes down*]

INNKEEPER: Here, here,
What's this, what's this, why are you standing idle?
They're calling for more wine!

SARAH: Let Leah serve them.
She likes their looks!

WIFE: Sarah!

SARAH [*sighs*]:Yes, mistress.

WIFE: Please, Sarah—we've talked like this so many times.

SARAH: Very well, mistress. But let her go first.
[*To Leah*]
Get up the stairs, you little soldier's comfort!
I hope he pinches you!

LEAH: Mistress, it's not my fault. Does Sarah have to—

WIFE: Oh, go, go—both of you!

[*They mutter and go upstairs*]

INNKEEPER: Well, that's a pretty little tempest for you.
You ought to beat the girl. She's insolent.
And shows it.

WIFE: We can't be too hard on her.
Her father's dead, her brother's in the hills,
And yet she used to be a merry child.
I can remember her when she was merry,
A long time since.

INNKEEPER: You always take their side
And yet, you'd think a self-respecting inn
Could have some decent and well-mannered maids!
But no such luck—sullens and sluts, the lot of them!
Give me a stool—I'm tired.

[*He sits, muttering*]

Say thirty dinners
And double for the prefect—and the wine—
Best, second best and common—h'm, not bad
But then—

[*Suddenly*]

Why do you sit there, staring at the fire,
So silent and so waiting and so still?

[*Unearthly music, very faint at first, begins with the
next speech and builds through the scene*]

WIFE: I do not know. I'm waiting.

INNKEEPER: Waiting for what?

WIFE: I do not know. For something new and strange,
Something I've dreamt about in some deep sleep,
Truer than any waking,
Heard about, long ago, so long ago,
In sunshine and the summer grass of childhood,
When the sky seems so near.

I do not know its shape, its will, its purpose
And yet all day its will has been upon me,
More real than any voice I ever heard,
More real than yours or mine or our dead child's,
More real than all the voices there upstairs,
Brawling above their cups, more real than light.
And there is light in it and fire and peace,
Newness of heart and strangeness like a sword,
And all my body trembles under it,
And yet I do not know.

INNKEEPER: You're tired, my dear.
Well, we shall sleep soon.

WIFE: No, I am not tired.
I am expectant as a runner is
Before a race, a child before a feast day,
A woman at the gates of life and death,
Expectant for us all, for all of us
Who live and suffer on this little earth
With such small brotherhood. Something begins.
Something is full of change and sparkling stars.
Something is loosed that changes all the world.

[*Music up and down*]

And yet—I cannot read it yet. I wait
And strive—and cannot find it.

[*A knock at the door*]

Hark? What's that?

INNKEEPER: They can't come in. I don't care who they
are.
We have no room.

[*Knock is repeated*]

WIFE: Go to the door!

[*He goes and opens the door*]

INNKEEPER: Well?

[*Strain of music*]

JOSEPH [*from outside*]: Is this the inn? Sir, we are travelers
And it is late and cold. May we enter?

WIFE [*eagerly*]: Who is it?

INNKEEPER [*to her*]: Just a pair of country people,
A woman and a man. I'm sorry for them
But—

JOSEPH: My wife and I are weary,
May we come in?

INNKEEPER: I'm sorry, my good man.
We have no room tonight. The prefect's orders.

JOSEPH: No room at all?

INNKEEPER: Now, now, it's not my fault.
You look like honest and well-meaning folk
And nobody likes turning trade away
But I'm not my own master. Not tonight.
It may be, in the morning—
[*He starts to close the door*]

WIFE: Wait!

INNKEEPER [*in a fierce whisper*]: Must you mix in this?

WIFE: Wait!
[*She goes to the door*]
Good sir, the enemy are in our house
And we—
[*She sees the Virgin, who does not speak throughout
this scene but is represented by music*]

WIFE: Oh.

[*Music*]

WIFE [*haltingly*]: I—did not see your wife. I did not know.

JOSEPH [*simply*]: Her name is Mary. She is near her time.

WIFE: Yes. Yes.

[*To the innkeeper*]

Go—get a lantern.

Quickly!

INNKEEPER: What?

WIFE: *Quickly!*

[*To Joseph and Mary*]

I—I once had a child.

We have no room. That's true.

And it would not be right. Not here. Not now.

Not with those men whose voices you can hear,

Voices of death and iron.—King Herod's voices.

Better the friendly beasts. What am I saying?

There is—we have a stable at the inn,

Safe from the cold, at least—and, if you choose,

You shall be very welcome. It is poor

But the poor share the poor their crumbs of bread

Out of God's hand, so gladly,

And that may count for something. Will you share it?

JOSEPH: Gladly and with great joy.

WIFE: The lantern, husband!

JOSEPH: Nay, I will take it. I can see the path.

Come!

[*Music up. Joseph and Mary go. Innkeeper and wife
watch them*]

INNKEEPER [*to wife*]: Well, I suppose that you must

have your way

And, any other night—They're decent people

Or seem to be—

WIFE: He has his arm about her, smoothing out

The roughness of the path for her.

INNKEEFER: —Although

They are not even people of our town,

As I suppose you know—
      WIFE: So rough a path to tread with weary feet!
      INNKEEPER: Come in.
      [*He shivers*]
Brr, there's a frost upon the air tonight.
I'm cold or—yes, I must be cold. That's it.
That's it, now, to be sure. Come, shut the door.
      WIFE: Something begins, begins;
Starlit and sunlit, something walks abroad
In flesh and spirit and fire.
Something is loosed to change the shaken world.
      [*Music up and down. A bell strikes the hour*]
      NARRATOR: The night deepens. The stars march in the
sky.
The prefect's men are gone. The inn is quiet
Save for the sleepy servants and their mistress,
Who clean the last soiled pots.
The innkeeper drowses before the fire.
But, in the street, outside—
      [*Music, changing into a shepherd's carol*]
      1ST SHEPHERD: As we poor shepherds watched by night
      CHORUS: With a hey, with a ho.
      1ST SHEPHERD: A star shone over us so bright
We left our flocks to seek its light
      CHORUS: In excelsis deo,
Gloria, gloria,
In excelsis deo.
      1ST SHEPHERD: We left our silly sheep to stray,
      CHORUS: With a hey, with a ho.
      1ST SHEPHERD: They'll think us no good shepherds,
they.
And yet we came a blessed way
      CHORUS: In excelsis deo,

Gloria, gloria,
In excelsis deo.

    1ST SHEPHERD: Now how may such a matter be?

    CHORUS: With a hey, with a ho.

    1ST SHEPHERD: That we of earth, poor shepherds we,
May look on Jesu's majesty?
And yet the star says—"It is He!"

    2ND SHEPHERD: It is He!

    3RD SHEPHERD: It is He!

    CHORUS: Sing excelsis deo!

Gloria, gloria
In excelsis deo!

    SARAH: Who sings so late? How can they sing so late?

    LEAH: I'll go and see.
Wait—I'll rub the windowpane.
It's rimed with frost.
    [*She looks out*]
They're shepherds from the hills.

    WIFE: Shepherds?

    LEAH: Yes, mistress. They have crooks and staves.
Their tattered cloaks are ragged on their backs.
Their hands are blue and stinging with the cold
And yet they all seem drunken, not with wine
But with good news. Their faces shine with it.

    WIFE: Cold—and so late. Poor creatures—call them in.
The prefect's men are gone.

    LEAH: Aye but—the master—

    WIFE: He's dozing. Do as I tell you.

    LEAH [*calling out*]: Come in—come in—tarry awhile
and rest!

    SHEPHERDS [*joyously*]: We cannot stay. We follow the
bright star.
Gloria, gloria

In excelsis deo!

WIFE: Where did they go? Would they not stay with us?
Not one?

LEAH: Mistress, they did not even look on me.
They looked ahead. They have gone toward the stable,
The stable of our inn.

LEAH [*excitedly*]: Aye—gone but—Mistress! Mistress!
Do you hear?

WIFE: Hear what?

LEAH: The tread of steeds on the hard ground,
Iron-hoofed, ringing clear—a company
That comes from out the East. I've never seen
Such things. I am afraid. These are great lords,
Great kings, with strange and memorable beasts,
And crowns upon their heads!

INNKEEPER [*waking*]: What's that? What's that?
Lords, nobles, kings, here in Bethlehem,
In our poor town? What fortune! O, what fortune!
Stand from the window there, you silly girl,
I'll speak to them!

[*He calls out*]
My gracious noble masters,
Worthy and mighty kings! Our humble inn
Is honored by your high nobility!
Come in—come in—we've fire and beds and wine!
Come in—come in—tarry awhile and rest!

KINGS' VOICES [*joyfully*]: We cannot stay! We follow the
bright star!
Gloria, gloria
In excelsis deo!

INNKEEPER: I do not understand it. They are gone.
They did not even look at me or pause
Though there's no other inn.

They follow the poor shepherds to the stable.

    WIFE: They would not tarry with us—no, not one.

    INNKEEPER: And yet—

    WIFE: Peace, husband. You know well enough

Why none would tarry with us.

And so do I. I lay awhile in sleep

And a voice said to me, "Gloria, gloria,

Gloria in excelsis deo.

The child is born, the child, the child is born!"

And yet I did not rise and go to him,

Though I had waited and expected long,

For I was jealous that my child should die

And her child live.

And so—I have my judgment. And it is just.

    INNKEEPER: Dreams.

    WIFE: Were they dreams, the shepherds and the kings?

Is it a dream, this glory that we feel

Streaming upon us—and yet not for us.

    LEAH: Now, mistress, mistress, 'tis my fault not yours.

You told me seek the strangers in the stable

And see they had all care but I—forgot.

    SARAH: Kissing your soldier!

    LEAH: Sarah!

    SARAH: I am sorry, Leah.

My tongue's too sharp. Mistress, the fault was mine.

You told me also and I well remembered

Yet did not go.

    WIFE: Sarah.

    SARAH: I did not go.

Brooding on mine own wrongs, I did not go.

It was my fault.

    INNKEEPER: If there was any fault, wife, it was mine.

I did not wish to turn them from my door

And yet—I know I love the chink of money,
Love it too well, the good, sound, thumping coin,
Love it—oh, God, since I am speaking truth,
Better than wife or fire or chick or child,
Better than country, better than good fame,
Would sell my people for it in the street,
Oh, for a price—but sell them.
And there are many like me. And God pity us.

    WIFE: God pity us indeed, for we are human,
And do not always see
The vision when it comes, the shining change,
Or, if we see it, do not follow it,
Because it is too hard, too strange, too new,
Too unbelievable, too difficult,
Warring too much with common, easy ways,
And now I know this, standing in this light,
Who have been half alive these many years,
Brooding on my own sorrow, my own pain,
Saying "I am a barren bough. Expect
Nor fruit nor blossom from a barren bough."
Life is not lost by dying! Life is lost
Minute by minute, day by dragging day,
In all the thousand, small, uncaring ways,
The smooth appeasing compromises of time,
Which are King Herod and King Herod's men,
Always and always. Life can be
Lost without vision but not lost by death,
Lost by not caring, willing, going on
Beyond the ragged edge of fortitude
To something more—something no man has seen.
You who love money, you who love yourself,
You who love bitterness, and I, who loved
And lost and thought I could not love again,

And all the people of this little town,
Rise up! The loves we had were not enough.
Something is loosed to change the shaken world,
And with it we must change!

[*The voice of Dismas, the thief, breaking in—a rather quizzical, independent voice*]

DISMAS: Now that's well said!

INNKEEPER: Who speaks there? Who are you?

DISMAS: Who? Oh, my name is Dismas. I'm a thief.
You know the starved, flea-bitten sort of boy
Who haunts dark alleyways in any town,
Sleeps on a fruit sack, runs from the police,
Begs what he can and—borrows what he must.
That's me!

INNKEEPER: How did you get here?

DISMAS: By the door, innkeeper,
The cellar door. The lock upon it's old.
I could pick locks like that when I was five.

INNKEEPER: What have you taken?

DISMAS: Nothing.
I tried the stable first—and then your cellar,
Slipped in, crept up, rolled underneath a bench,
While all your honest backs were turned—and then—

WIFE: And then?

DISMAS: Well—something happened. I don't know what.
I didn't see your shepherds or your kings,
But, in the stable, I did see the child,
Just through a crack in the boards—one moment's space.
That's all that I can tell you.

[*Passionately*]

Is he for me as well? Is he for me?

WIFE: For you as well.

DISMAS: Is he for all of us?

There are so many of us, worthy mistress,
Beggars who show their sores and ask for alms,
Women who cough their lungs out in the cold,
Slaves—oh, I've been one!—thieves and runagates
Who knife each other for a bite of bread,
Having no other way to get the bread,
—The vast sea of the wretched and the poor,
Whose murmur comes so faintly to your ears
In this fine country.
Has he come to all of us
Or just to you?

> WIFE: To every man alive.

> DISMAS: I wish I could believe.

> SARAH [*scornfully*]: And, if you did,

No doubt you'd give up thieving!

> DISMAS: Gently, lady, gently.

Thieving's my trade—the only trade I know.
But, if it were true,
If he had really come to all of us—
I say, to all of us—
Then, honest man or thief,
I'd hang upon a cross for him!

> [*A shocked pause. The others mutter*]

> DISMAS: Would *you*?

> [*Another pause*]

I see that I've said something you don't like,
Something uncouth and bold and terrifying,
And yet, I'll tell you this:
It won't be till each one of us is willing,
Not you, not me, but every one of us,
To hang upon a cross for every man
Who suffers, starves and dies,
Fight his sore battles as they were our own,

And help him from the darkness and the mire,
That there will be no crosses and no tyrants,
No Herods and no slaves.
    [*Another pause*]
Well, it was pleasant, thinking things might be so.
And so I'll say farewell. I've taken nothing.
And he was a fair child to look on.
    WIFE: Wait!
    DISMAS: Why? What is it you see there, by the window?
    WIFE: The dawn, the common day,
The ordinary, poor and mortal day.
The shepherds and the kings have gone away.
The great angelic visitors are gone.
He is alone. He must not be alone.
    INNKEEPER: I do not understand you, wife.
    DISMAS: Nor I.
. . . . WIFE: Do you not see, because I see at last?
Dismas, the thief, is right.
He comes to all of us or comes to none.
Not to my heart in joyous recompense
For what I lost—not to your heart or yours,
But to the ignorant heart of all the world,
So slow to alter, so confused with pain.
Do you not see he must not be alone?
    INNKEEPER: I think that I begin to see. And yet—
    WIFE: We are the earth his word must sow like wheat
And, if it finds no earth, it cannot grow.
We are his earth, the mortal and the dying,
Led by no star—the sullen and the slut,
The thief, the selfish man, the barren woman,
Who have betrayed him once and will betray him,
Forget his words, be great a moment's space
Under the strokes of chance,

And then sink back into our small affairs.
And yet, unless *we* go, his message fails.

LEAH: Will he bring peace, will he bring brotherhood?

WIFE: He would bring peace, he would bring brotherhood
And yet he will be mocked at in the street.

SARAH: Will he slay King Herod
And rule us all?

WIFE: He will not slay King Herod. He will die.
There will be other Herods, other tyrants,
Great wars and ceaseless struggles to be free,
Not always won.

INNKEEPER: These are sad tidings of him.

WIFE: No, no—they are glad tidings of great joy,
Because he brings man's freedom in his hands,
Not as a coin that may be spent or lost
But as a living fire within the heart,
Never quite quenched—because he brings to all,
The thought, the wish, the dream of brotherhood,
Never and never to be wholly lost,
The water and the bread of the oppressed,
The stay and succor of the resolute,
The harness of the valiant and the brave,
The new word that has changed the shaken world.
And, though he die, his word shall grow like wheat
And every time a child is born,
In pain and love and freedom hardly won,
Born and gone forth to help and aid mankind,
There will be women with a right to say
"Gloria, gloria in excelsis deo!
A child is born!"

SARAH: Gloria!

LEAH: Gloria!

WIFE: Come, let us go. What can we bring to him?
What mortal gifts?

LEAH [*shyly*]: I have a ribbon. It's my prettiest.
It is not much but—he might play with it.

SARAH: I have a little bell my father gave me.
It used to make me merry. I have kept it.
I—he may have it.

DISMAS: My pocket's empty and my rags are bare.
But I can sing to him. That's what I'll do
And—if he needs a thief to die for him—

INNKEEPER: I would give all my gold.
I will give my heart.

WIFE: And I my faith through all the years and years,
Though I forget, though I am led astray,
Though, after this I never see his face,
I will give all my faith.
Come, let us go,
We, the poor earth but we, the faithful earth,
Not yet the joyful, not yet the triumphant,
But faithful, faithful, through the mortal years!
Come!

[*Music begins*]

DISMAS [*sings*]: Come, all ye faithful.

INNKEEPER: Joyful and triumphant.

WOMEN: Come ye, O come ye to Bethlehem!

[*Their voices rise in chorus in "Come, all ye faithful."
The chorus and the music swell.*]

(CURTAIN)

YOUR ARMY

This script was one of thirteen programs which were produced in co-operation with the United States government and broadcast over the four major networks on thirteen consecutive Saturday evenings beginning February 14, 1944. The series was heard over more than six hundred radio stations in this country and was short-waved abroad.

The principal voice in *Your Army* was that of Tyrone Power. The program was directed by Norman Corwin; the music was composed and conducted by Morton Gould, and the program produced by H. L. McClinton.

YOUR ARMY

[*Music: Bugle call sounding assembly. Bugle call continues in background or is picked up as musical theme through this sequence*]

NARRATOR: This is the Army! Ground, Air and Supply. Infantry!

VOICES: Fall in! Fall in! Fall in!

[*Shuffle of men's feet*]

NARRATOR: Cavalry!

OFFICER: As skirmishers—Gallop—Follow me!

[*Hoofbeats*]

NARRATOR: Artillery!

OFFICER: March order!

[*Roll of wheels*]

CHORUS [*singing*]: Oh, it's hi, hi, hee in the field artilleree. Shout out your numbers loud and strong—one! two!

VOICES: One, two, three, four! One, two, three, four!

VOICES: Fall in, fall in, fall in!

NARRATOR: Tanks!

TANK COMMANDER: Let her roll!

[*Clank of tanks*]

NARRATOR: Pursuit command, interceptor* command, bomber command!

[*Roar of plane motors*]

SPOTTER [*filter*]: Enemy planes sighted at twelve thousand feet, area seven! Twelve thousand feet, area seven! Proceed to engage enemy!

1ST VOICE: Contact!

2ND VOICE: Follow me!

3RD VOICE: Deflection one-twenty—On Number One— Open fire, Battery, Four thousand. Open fire!

NARRATOR: This is the Army! Engineers, machine-gunners, ordnance, quartermaster, mechanized and armored units, ski troops and parachute troops—everything that'll fly or roll or shoot—Thirty-four divisions, Nine corps, Four field armies training—this is the United States Army—one million, seven hundred thousand men!

[*Music: Up to climax with plenty of brass, then out*]

NARRATOR [*resuming more quietly; under this, spot muted assembly call*]: Sure, we know. We know this is the army. Our army. A people's army, raised and equipped and run by a free people, made up of Bill Jones and Bennie Cohen and Stan Woczinski, Burt Anderson and Charlie Pappas, the kid who dropped out of college when he heard about Pearl Harbor, and the blond kid who used to pop sodas at the Combination Drugstore last year. That's our army—and we know that. But how much do we know?

[*Bugle call—assembly*]

NARRATOR: What's an army about? What's it for—a free

people's army? [*More quietly*] Let's go back just a minute and see—go back to the roots of the nation.

CLERK [*reading; music in*]: Article Two. A well-regulated militia being necessary to the security of a free state, the right of the people to keep and bear arms shall not be infringed.

[*Music out*]

NARRATOR: That's the second amendment to the Constitution. The men who passed it had been through a long hard war to make their free state. They knew how that state must be kept. And Washington said—

WASHINGTON: "To be prepared for war is one of the most effectual means of preserving peace. A free people ought not only to be armed but disciplined."

NARRATOR: Washington spoke from experience. He'd seen his men starve—he'd seen them chased like foxes— Here's one of his generals, writing a letter home—

GENERAL: ". . . The whole army has now gone into winter cantonments excepting General Nixon's and my brigade who are now in the field (eight hundred of my men without shoes or stockings) enjoying the sweets of a winter campaign while the worthy and virtuous citizens of America are enduring the hardships, toils and fatigues incident to parlors with good fires and sleeping on beds of down . . ."

NARRATOR: Forget it? Why, of course. It happened over one hundred and fifty years ago and we won that one, didn't we? Ye-es. But let's just hear one more witness—the father of the idol of the South—the cavalryman they called Light-Horse Harry Lee.

LEE: "A government is the murderer of its citizens which sends them to the field uninformed and untaught, where they are to meet men of the same age, mechanized by education and discipline for battle."

NARRATOR: Pretty grim, isn't it? Pretty businesslike? And—pretty contemporary? Are you listening, gentlemen of Congress?

[*Whistle and blast of bomb*]

NARRATOR: That was Batavia—falling. [*Pause*] Are you listening—you good, decent, honest, peace-minded Americans—and you're all of that—who didn't see and couldn't see why our country needed a real army? [*Change of tone*] We forgot, of course. We're apt to forget, between wars, forget the voices and the warnings. We cut the standing army down to eighty men, right after the Revolution. And in 1812 we fought another war—and we were invaded and our capital was burned—but we won that one. And in 'forty-six and sixty-one we fought other wars—

[*Music: Motif*]

SERGEANT: Captain Blake—hey, Captain Blake!

CAPTAIN: Yes, sergeant. What's the trouble?

SERGEANT: They's two hundred men with their rifles just come down here from the hills of Kentucky! They all want to enlist at once and I just can't do a thing with them!

CAPTAIN: Well, swear them in. Swear them in.

SERGEANT: Hell, they don't want to be swore in! They just want to know where this place called Matamoros is and how soon can they get [*fading*] there and start shootin'—

[*Music: Out*]

NARRATOR: Yes, that's the spirit—that's always been the spirit. And, in 'sixty-one—

CHORUS [*singing*]: We are a band of brothers, devoted to the soil,

Fighting for the property we gained by honest toil,

And when our rights were threatened, we loudly cried hurrah,
Hurrah, hurrah for the bonny blue flag that boasts but a single star!

CHORUS [*cutting in*]: We're coming, Father Abraham, three hundred thousand more . . . [*Fading*]

NARRATOR: A good spirit—a fine spirit—no better fighters on earth than the men who fought with Scott and Taylor, Lee and Grant. And the Regular Army, small, handicapped, kicked around in peacetime like a football, did its job without brag or bluster and did it well. But the boys who died at Matamoros and First Bull Run died only too often as Light-Horse Harry Lee said they shouldn't die —uninformed and untrained. They died at Chickamauga, in 'ninety-eight—of fever—they died on San Juan Hill.

[*Strain of music*]

They went to France in 'seventeen and 'eighteen—two million of them first and last. We know what they did there.

The German General Staff said we couldn't put an army in the field—we put two million men. They broke the enemy's front and went to the Rhine—

[*Triumphant music*]

And then we demobilized. Glad to. Wasn't the world at peace?

Well—you know what happened.

But, this time, we did make some plans. For the first time in history, we raised a draft army before war fell on us. Raised it fair and square, by lot and law, raised it out of just the same sort of Americans who fought at Trenton and Cerro Gordo, Chancellorsville and Cantigny. And we've got it now—and it's working!

Forget the past for a moment—forget even the heroic names of the past! This is war! And this is now. Not yesterday—not Gettysburg or the Marne—the Alamo or Château-Thierry—but *now!*

[*Music: Clash of music, fading into a slow, spinning sound*]

NARRATOR: That's a map—a map of 'the world—the whole round globe of earth. It's in the office of the Chief of Staff at Washington—General George C. Marshall. He is the tenth man in all our history to wear the four silver stars of a full general. He is the first American general who ever had to plan a grand strategy that took in all the world.

It's a quiet room, this central brain-cell of the Army. The men who go in and out of it wear uniforms—the man who sits at the big desk wears a uniform. Otherwise, it's rather like any executive office. There's no spur-jingling or table-pounding. The papers flow in and out and the calls go in and out, night and day—from the three great branches of the Army—Ground, Air and Supply.

Red tape? Brass hats?

I thought you'd ask about that. We're funny people, that way, when it comes to our army. We wouldn't hire a lawyer who'd never been to law school. We wouldn't employ a surgeon who'd never done an appendectomy. But if a man has been schooled and trained all his life in the theory and practice of war—why, he's a red-tape brass hat and everybody's free to criticize. And yet, war is also a profession. Ask the Axis. I wonder just who are the red-tape brass hats—MacArthur, the West Point graduate, who sat in this room once—or the country-club strategist who tells us all how to win the war over cocktails? Marshall, the V.M.I. graduate—or the congressman from South Overcoat who never fired a gun? Yes, I wonder sometimes.

We pay General Marshall eight thousand dollars a year.

[*Whistle*]

That's not big money, is it? And the same to Mac-Arthur for holding off 200,000 Japs on Luzon. But they aren't kicking about the pay. They're satisfied.

And what do they do to earn their pay? Wheie do the plans get executed? What sort of news comes into the quiet room? Let's listen a minute—short-wave—

[*Crackle of short-wave*]

PRIVATE: "Hello, mom! Hello, dad! This is Jimmy—Jimmy. I'm talking from Ulster. We just landed. Well, I guess I was the first guy ashore so the old man said I could broadcast. Yeah, we're fine and the folks are swell here. Yeah, I got my clean socks on. Yeah, remember me to Millie and the boys—"

[*Crackle out*]

NARRATOR: That was a private in the United States Army, talking from Northern Ireland. And here—

CORPORAL [*writing letter*]: "Dear Susy:—

"I hope this finds you O.K. just as it leaves me. It's cold around here. But a guy who's used to Minnesota can't kick. Pretty scenery, too, though they farm different. Well, we've got a job to do and I guess we mean to do it. All the same, Susy, I'd kind of like to hear from you. Your last letter was swell but I ain't had one since. You might write a guy once in a while—"

NARRATOR: That was a Corporal attached to our task-force in Iceland. Now—

[*Voice recites latest Philippine communiqué*]

NARRATOR: That was MacArthur's men—tonight—from the foxholes of Bataan. Still holding.

And here—

VOICE [*filter*]: Reporting to Chief of Staff. Reporting to

Chief of Staff. American task force B safely landed at Rendezvous K in South Pacific—

NARRATOR: Ireland—Iceland—Luzon—Batavia—Alaska the Caribbean—halfway round the world, American troops are marching—American planes are flying— But why? Why? We're defending ourselves—aren't we? We built an army for defense—didn't we? So why do we have to fight all over the map?

Listen—here's your answer.

[*Roar of airplane motors*]

NARRATOR: Hear that? That's the B-19—the biggest bomber yet built in the U. S. A. So big that when the pilot wants to rev up a motor, he doesn't do it himself—he phones someone else to do it. So big she can carry eighteen tons of bombs from New York to Athens and back—seven thousand miles under her own power. So big that she just got finished. And already outmoded.

COLD VOICE [*echo*]: Outmoded.

NARRATOR: Yes. But we learned a lot from making her and on the drawing boards now are airplane motors that develop even more thousands of horsepower. They'll be made and they'll fly the planes and keep 'em flying. How far? Maybe halfway round the world. The world has shrunk like a squeezed orange—old tools of war are obsolete.

COLD VOICE [*echo*]: Obsolete.

NARRATOR: You can bomb Detroit from Brest. You can bomb Pearl Harbor from the wastes of the Pacific. You can bomb Philadelphia from Iceland. And what stops the bombers? You have to have bases to stop them—you have to have hangars and ground crews and landing fields where your own planes can take off. You have to have guns and men to protect those bases.

BRITISH PILOT: Last night—I was over Berlin. Tonight

—I'm here in Boston. Odd sensation—rather. But it happened. I caught the ferry plane.

NARRATOR: That British pilot—you've read about him in the papers. Last night—Berlin—tonight—Boston. And that's just the air—just one huge phase of modern war. What about the ground?

GERMAN [*filter*]: Captain Hauptmann, Second Tank Group, reporting to Headquarters. During the last eight hours the group has advanced sixty-three miles.

NARRATOR: That was a single German tank unit in the Battle of France. In the last war, an advance of sixty-three miles usually meant weeks of fighting, the lives of thousands of men. But this is mechanized war—modern war—war of rupture—war that flies through the air at four hundred miles an hour—war that spills and runs like quicksilver on lands and homes that only yesterday were peaceful and miles away from the guns. War fought around the curve of earth—quick-hitting, hard-striking, sudden, deadly. Call the roll! Have we got the tools to fight it? What tools have we got? What machines?

[*Sound: Mechanical noise*]

VOICE: Well, here s one of them—mechanical range computer—what the boys call a juke-box in antiaircraft. Kind of brainy old buzzard. Hooks up with the range finder and the sound locater and the searchlights—figures out the speed and altitude and range of enemy planes and then sets your guns so your shells burst on the target. Yep, all by its little self, once you turn those wheels. And—it doesn't make mistakes. When you start coming over, Mr. Hitler—just remember the juke-box boys!

NARRATOR: Modern war—war of machines and skills— or dials and calibrations and micrometers—war we're able to fight because we know about them—because when we want, we can make the best machines in the world—You've heard about our bomb-sight—well—

[*Roar of airplane motor*]

VOICE: That it?

2ND VOICE: Yep. That's the baby. And she's everything they say.

VOICE: Looks good.

2ND VOICE: Looks good? Listen, soldier, with that little hipper-dipper you can drop a bomb in a pickle barrel once you've got the know-how. That's how Kelly and his bombardier sank the *Haruna*—and they weren't shooting wild— they knew how. Now just take a look at the—

[*Very big noise of guns*]

NARRATOR: Ouch. What's that?

VOICE: One fifty-five millimeter gun, sir. [*Gun explosion*] Cost—fifty thousand dollars. Weight—thirty thousand pounds. Fires a ninety-five pound shell nearly fifteen miles. But mobile—you can haul it around by truck or tractor, camouflage it, and use it right behind your front line. We call this one Kate Smith. She's a honey. And we're going to need a lot of them.

NARRATOR: Hear that, you folks in the shops? How many Kate Smiths are coming off the production line? How many can you make?

[*Rip of machine-gun fire*]

VOICE: Fifty-caliber machine gun—air-cooled—automatic—used by motorized infantry—terrific hitting power—

NARRATOR: But how many? How many? A triangular division needs plenty of machine guns. And every production day counts—in this kind of war. We could show you the light tanks and the mediums, the range finders and the fuse timers, and all the tools of modern war. We could show you the jeep—come in, jeep!

[*Music: Jeep motif in*]

JEEP [*rather screwy and metallic*]: Jeep!

NARRATOR: How fast can you travel, jeep?

JEEP: Sixty miles an hour on good roads and whatever you can stand on bad ones. My mother was a tin Lizzie and my father was a jack rabbit. I'll cart four men and their stuff and I'll tow machine guns and mortars. I'm a cross-country runner and a bulldog and an armor-plated, hell-before-breakfast get-there—give me room! I've got the jump of a flea and the guts of a terrier and I'm harder to kill than an army mule. That's me—jeep!

NARRATOR: Thanks, jeep.

JEEP: Call me scout car. Can't a guy have a little dignity when he's on the air?

NARRATOR: Okay, scout car. Dismissed.

JEEP: Jeep!

[*Music: Jeep motif concludes*]

NARRATOR: Sure, we could show you all those. We could show you other things and take all night showing them—Because, for every man we put in the front line, there are something like eight men behind him—and, if those men aren't on the job, the man at the front is out of luck. The people we're going to talk to don't always get their names in the papers.

[*Cast and sound: ad libs sneak in*]

NARRATOR: But if they weren't on the job, we wouldn't have an army. What's your job, soldier?

COOK: Me? I cook for the Fourth Battery. And, boy, can those buzzards eat!

NARRATOR: H'm. Must be a pretty soft job—just cooking for a gang of soldiers.

COOK: Sez you. You just listen to 'em howl when the chow don't suit them. Not that I blame them. It takes food in your guts to make a soldier—and that's my job.

NARRATOR: Well, anyhow, it sounds like a nice, easy detail.

COOK: Sez you. You ever up in the Argonne?

NARRATOR: No.

COOK: Well, I was. Nice quiet place to cook for a battery, the Argonne. Just as nice and quiet and safe as a four-alarm fire. I drew three months hospital, and it wasn't because I got wounded opening tin cans.

NARRATOR: Thanks, soldier, and—oh, by the way, I've got a message for you. The sergeant said to be sure to ask you how you were fixed for lemon extract.

COOK [*roaring*]: Lemon extract! Why, the slabsided son of a— Lemon extract! Say, you get out of my kitchen [*fading*] before I take this cleaver and—

NARRATOR: I wonder what made him so sore? Didn't mean to do it—you make a battery cook sore and you're in for trouble. Now here's somebody with a hat cord I don't recognize—maroon and white. Excuse me, soldier—could you tell me just why you've got a different hat cord from these other men?

MEDICAL: Medical Corps, sir.

NARRATOR: Oh, that it? Medical Corps.

MEDICAL: Yes, sir. I'm a pill roller. Stretcher-bearer in action. This is my field kit.

NARRATOR: H'm. You seem to be pretty well supplied.

MEDICAL: Have to be, sir. Casualties. Have to be prepared.

NARRATOR: And tell me—do you go out under fire?

MEDICAL: Wouldn't do much good if I didn't, sir. The

faster you can get the wounded out, the better chance they've got.

NARRATOR: Thank you. And you?

SIGNAL: First sergeant, Signal Corps. Used to be a telephone lineman. That's my job.

NARRATOR: I thought nowadays it was all radio.

SIGNAL: Oh, we've got good radio. Got the walkie-talkie —that's a two-way radio outfit one man can carry on his back. Used for liaison and communication. But we still need telephones and installations. We still need men to carry the lines to the front—repair them—keep them working no matter if all hell's breaking. This kind of army needs both wireless and wire—and men who can work them both.

NARRATOR: I can see that. And you?

QUARTERMASTER: I'm a quartermaster sergeant. Sure, we count blankets, we count shoes, we hand out the rations. Or that's all they'll tell you we do. If the grub doesn't get to the railhead—if it doesn't get from there to the cooks— the guy up front is going to go pretty hungry. If his shoes don't fit and he goes lame—he's a soldier out of action. That's our job—to see he's clothed and fed. May not sound like much. But we're clothing and feeding one million seven hundred thousand men.

NARRATOR: Thank you. Just a few of the skills and services that go to the making of an army. And right where the shooting starts—

Would you come up to the mike a minute, soldier with the blue hat cord and the crossed rifles on your collar? Who are you and what's your job?

INFANTRY: I'm infantry. I'm Private Dogface, private one million, draft number 2985, dog-tag number 893-247. Otherwise, I'm just the guy who occupies ground. They land me in planes from the air and they shoot me up to the front in trucks and scout cars . . . but a lot of the time, still, I walk—yes, even with all the wheels and machines of modern war.

I walk and I creep and I dig and I burrow and I wiggle ahead. I take cover and I creep from cover and I hold the line. I hide all day in the foxholes under the bombings, and last out. I marched with the Continentals and I marched with the Army of the Valley, and in France I went ahead through the wheat, and I'm still marching. I'm blind without planes and you've got to give me planes—I can't fight tanks with my hands and you've got to give me tanks—I'm not artillery and you've got to give me guns—but, when all's said and done, I'm the guy who holds the ground. I'm not just a foot-slogger with a rifle in this new army—I'm a member of a combat team, trained like a football squad and with plenty of razzle-dazzle stuff—the Notre Dame stuff and the Army stuff and the Rose Bowl stuff of modern war. [*Sneak music*] But my first job and my last is to take the ground and hold the ground. I may do it forty miles an hour—I may do it two miles a day. I'm going to be cold and wet and hungry and thirsty and tired beyond tiredness. I'm going to see my friends die and hear the wounded cry out like a whispering field. But I'm going ahead and I'm going to win—the ground-gripper—the infantry—Private Dogface of the U.S. Army.

[*Music: Up to a finish that means business*]

NARRATOR: And—what are *we* going to do, sitting here at our radios? Squabble some more? Write letters to the papers? Hoard sugar? Curse out the government? Spread the lies that divide a people? Fold up in a chilly sweat every time there's bad news? There's bad news now, and there's going to be bad news for quite a while. The Army knows that. Our enemies aren't pushovers—they are skillful, savage and relentless. They have trained for years for this chance to enslave the world—and that's just what they mean to do. They'll use every trick and tool. On the other hand—they aren't supermen—they didn't come down from Mars. They can be licked and they will be licked—by men. Not by men without machines or by machines without men —but by men fighting for freedom with the right sort of tools in their hands. And—paste this one in your hat. It wasn't just the snow and the cold and the mud that bogged down the German drive in Russia—it was a fighting army and a fighting people. It wasn't just tradition and Magna Carta that stopped the Luftwaffe cold in the Battle of London—it was a fighting air force and a fighting people. We've got the fighting army and it's going to fight—all the way around the curve of earth. Men are going to die—very good men are going to die.

They're going to die in the jungles for the shape of a Virginia field and the crossroads store back home—they're going to die in the cold, for the clear air of Montana and the smell of a New York street and the church where they used to go, if they went to church . . . for some things they learned at school and for some things we've all of us learned—for three words cut in gray rock, "Duty, Honor, Country"—and for an idea called freedom. I'm not going to use the big words. I'm not going to talk about "sacrifice" or "in vain." We are going to know such sacrifices as we have not known since Valley Forge—and, unless we win this war, even that will be in vain. It's you that I'm talking to—and you and you—all over America. We've got a fighting army—let's show them a fighting people! [*With change of tone*] You see, armies differ. In some countries, an army means a steely political machine, dominating the government, trampling on the rights of the people. What's our army? Let's hear from one of its historians. [*Smack of lips*]

A DELIBERATE VOICE: It has a soul of its own. It is nothing in itself; it is everything as an organ of government. It has no political aims, no political ambitions. Its commander in chief is a civilian. It is the people's army and theirs alone.

NARRATOR: In some countries, an army is run by a [*fade in steps*] heel-clicking military caste.

VOICE: Get into the gutter, you civilian swine! Don't you know the sidewalk is for officers?

2ND VOICE: Yes, captain. Certainly, captain. Zu befehl, Herr Kapitan.

[*Fade out steps*]

NARRATOR: No—that isn't our army and it never has been. We have our training school for regular officers— West Point. Money won't get you into West Point and neither will the Social Register. No graduate of West Point has ever tried to upset the political system of this country —no graduate of West Point has ever tried to build up a ruling military caste. They are men who do their hard jobs for less than civilian wages—and when they retire, for a few of them, there's a medal in a box, and a flag hung up on the wall of a cramped suburban apartment. And, for others, there are the graves—the graves in Arlington, at Soissons, in the cemetery at Manila, in the unmarked ground—the graves marked—

VOICE: "Here lies an American soldier known only to God."

NARRATOR: But meanwhile they do their job and they live up to their specifications—"Duty, Honor, Country." That's our ruling military caste.

[*Music: "Army Blue"*]

NARRATOR: And the others—well, you know them. The lawyer, the doctor, the florist, the man you take the five-ten with—the hacker, the clerk, the farmer—everybody who's got somewhere a piece of paper with the seal of the United States on it and the words "Honorable Discharge." That's our army—the people's army—and their sons are in it to-day.

[*Music: Start music, maybe "Stars and Stripes Forever"*]

NARRATOR: It's an old army and a new one. It goes back to the cross-belted Continentals and the farmers who held their fire at Bunker Hill. It's Dan Morgan's riflemen and Stonewall Jackson's foot-cavalry and the Rainbow Division and the men who hold Luzon. It's the dandy silk-stocking outfits from the cities and the sergeant with half a dozen hash marks, the shavetail fresh from the Point with his class ring shiny on his finger and Private Perkey of the Kitchen Police. It's an army that calls its leaders Marse Robert and Old Jack, Ulysses and Old Ironpants and the Green Hornet—An army with its tongue in its cheek and its gun in its hands. A disciplined army—you bet—but our own kind of discipline—an army that takes to machines like a duck to water—the fighting army of the American people, of the people, by the people and for the people, first, last, and all the time!

[*Music: Up and out*]

NARRATOR: Are you back of it? Listen!

[*Music: In*]

CHORUS: This is the Army,
This is your Army,
The United States Army,
Let's go!
We've got the stuff and we've got the poise

And we've got the axe for the Axis boys,
It's a great big axe for the Great Big Noise,
Hear it come, brother! Told you so!

For we are the Army.
The leather-necked Army,
The United States Army,
That's why
With the jeeps and the peeps and the bombers too
The tanks and the ranks and the army stew,
We're going to see this damn thing through,
Sock it home, brother! That's the guy!
We're fighting for freedom,
And folks we remember,
The girls we remember,
The land of the free,
It's a long tough march and a long tough war
But we're going to get what we're fighting for
And it's Hitler's hide on the old barn door,
United States Army!
That's me!
    [*Music: Up to climax*]

(CURTAIN)

TOWARD THE CENTURY OF MODERN MAN

PRAYER

On United Nations Flag Day, June 14, 1942, there was broadcast over the NBC Network *Toward the Century of the Common Man,* a script especially written for the occasion by George Faulkner. Stephen Vincent Benét was asked to write the closing speech for this script, which is here reprinted.

Following immediately after the close of this declaration, there was broadcast on the same program the transcribed Flag Day speech of President Roosevelt, who during the course of his address read the Prayer that was written by Stephen Vincent Benét at the request of the Librarian of Congress, Archibald McLeish.

Included in the all-star cast were Charles Boyer, Joseph Calleia, Ronald Coleman, Melville Cooper, Donald Dickson, Peter Lorre, Thomas Mitchell, Alla Nazimova and Maria Ouspenskaya. The music was composed by Robert Armstrong and Kurt Weil, with the orchestra conducted by Mr. Weil. The co-producers for NBC were Calvin Kuhl and David Elton.

TOWARD THE CENTURY OF
MODERN MAN

PRINCIPAL VOICE: I've been known by many names, in many times and places, I crawled out of the sea and the mud, long ages ago, and the gods of the thunder and lightning looked at me and said, "That's a queer, new fish. He'll never last on land." I hid in the forests, small and frightened, and the dinosaurs clanked around and said, "Who's this impractical dreamer? We'll eat him alive—he's got nothing but hands and a brain." But they left their bones in the rock and I lasted them out and went on. I crept out of caves toward the sunlight—and I built the free cities of Greece and the law that was Rome. I gathered the wisdom of China and I sent a word crying through Palestine—a word that cries through the centuries to all men and nations. "There is neither Jew nor Greek, there is neither bond nor free, but we are all brothers." And that word goes on.

I have dreamed many times. I found a new world, in small ships—and none but the Believers believed in me when I first dared that unknown West. When I wrote "All men are created free and equal," few believed at first. But, slowly, many believed, and many followed Jefferson. I shivered and prayed at Valley Forge, and my prayer was answered. When I stood at Gettysburg and spoke over the graves, few believed. But the Union lives and shall live— and government of the people, by the people, for the people, shall not perish from the earth.

Yes, I have been called many names—San Martín and Simon Bolívar, Hampden and Juarez, Rousseau and Socrates. I have spilt my blood in the streets of Paris and Athens and Moscow—I have grown as an oak tree grows from the roots of English law. I have been a preacher named Paul and a railsplitter named Abe Lincoln. I have been called a weakling and a fool, but it is the brave and the sane who follow me first and always.

Always, first, there has been the dream and the men who were willing to die for it. I call forth the dream and the men—I call them forth from all nations, when man stands up on his feet and looks his fate in the eyes. Only yesterday, on Corregidor, my name was Bill Smith from Ohio—and Jesu Maria Garcia was my brother's name. We had a rock to defend, and we defended it. And the name of that rock is Liberty, and in that name I speak.

For Liberty can be lost by the practical men whose hearts are too shrunken to contain it. Liberty can be bartered away by the greedy minds who cannot see beyond their own day. Liberty can be stolen away by the robber and the brute. But Liberty grows like grass in the hearts of the common people, from the blood of their martyrs. And the tyrants rage and are gone, but the dream and the deed endure—and I endure.

It is I who command men and win battles. I have called them forth in the past, I am calling them forth to-day. I call the brave to the battle-line, I call the sane to the council—I call the free millions of earth to the century ahead—the century of the common man, established by you, the people. *For this world cannot endure, half slave and half free!*

My name is FREEDOM and my command today is . . .
CHORUS [*unison*]: Unite!

PRAYER

God of the free, we pledge our hearts and lives today to the cause of all free mankind.

Grant us victory over the tyrants who would enslave all free men and nations. Grant us faith and understanding to cherish all those who fight for freedom as if they were our brothers. Grant us brotherhood in hope and union, not only for the space of this bitter war, but for the days to come which shall and must unite all the children of earth.

Our earth is but a small star in the great universe. Yet of it we can make, if we choose, a planet unvexed by war, untroubled by hunger or fear, undivided by senseless distinctions of race, color or theory. Grant us that courage and foreseeing to begin this task today that our children and our children's children may be proud of the name of man.

The spirit of man has awakened and the soul of man has gone forth. Grant us the wisdom and the vision to comprehend the greatness of man's spirit, that suffers and endures so hugely for a goal beyond his own brief span. Grant us honor for our dead who died in the faith, honor for our living who work and strive for the faith, redemption and security for all captive lands and peoples. Grant us patience with the deluded and pity for the betrayed. And grant us the skill and valor that shall cleanse the world of oppression and the old base doctrine that the strong must eat the weak because they are strong.

Yet most of all grant us brotherhood, not only for this day but for all our years—a brotherhood not of words but of acts and deeds. We are all of us children of earth—grant us that simple knowledge. If our brothers are oppressed, then we are oppressed. If they hunger, we hunger. If their freedom is taken away, our freedom is not secure. Grant us a common faith that man shall know bread and peace— that he shall know justice and righteousness, freedom and security, an equal opportunity and an equal chance to do his best, not only in our own lands, but throughout the world. And in that faith let us march toward the clean world our hands can make. Amen.